101 WAYS TO
Juice It!

The Complete Whole Grain Cookbook

Wholesome Harvest

101 WAYS TO Juice It!

LUSCIOUS RECIPES AND THE BEST AND MOST COMPREHENSIVE GUIDE TO FRUIT AND VEGETABLE JUICING

Carol Gelles

HarperCollins*Publishers*

HarperCollins books may be purchased for educational, business, or sales promotional use. For information please write: Special Markets Department, HarperCollins Publishers, Inc., 10 East 53rd Street, New York, NY 10022.

Designed by Jessica Shatan

Library of Congress Cataloging-in-Publication Data

Gelles, Carol.
  101 Ways to juice it! : luscious recipes and the best and most comprehensive guide to fruit and vegetable juicing/Carol Gelles.—1st ed.
      p.   cm.
  Includes bibliographical references and index.
  ISBN 0-06-016969-9
  1. Fruit juices.   2. Vegetable juices.   I. Title.
TX811.G36   1993
641.8'75—dc20   92-53372

93 94 95 96 97 DT/HC 10 9 8 7 6 5 4 3

For: Mom, Dad, and Sherry
Randy Kraft, Girl Reporter
Paula and Poppy

CONTENTS

ACKNOWLEDGMENTS

This book would never have happened without two very special people. Susan Friedland, my editor, who originated the idea for this project and then gave me free rein in the execution of the idea—thanks.

My outstanding agent, Judith Weber, who is always available to me and whose input to all my projects has been invaluable and, last but not least, whose matchmaking was instrumental in my writing this book.

Special thanks to the manufacturers of the juice extractors, who offered information as well as machines for my comparative tests, and the spas that chose to participate in this project with information and recipes.

Apologies to my dad, who always seemed to get the yucky juices to taste (the ones that didn't make it into the book).

And to my friends and family who, as ever, are always there.

PART I

All About Juicing

Getting Started

WHO SHOULD JUICE?

Everyone benefits from drinking fresh juices. They are especially valuable to people on the run who don't regularly eat enough fruits and
vegetables.

3

The latest government findings recommend three to five servings
daily of vegetables and two to four servings daily of fruits. Although
these amounts don't sound like a lot, many of us don't even meet the
minimum recommendations. Juicing is an easy and quick way to help
meet at least the minimum requirements for fruits and vegetables.

But juice is not a panacea. For good health you need to include
fiber in your diet. Whole fruits and vegetables are excellent sources of
fiber, and the juicing process discards this valuable nutrient. So unless
you are eating plenty of whole grains and beans, you must still follow
your mother's advice and eat (not just drink) your vegetables (and
fruits).

JUICING—THE PROS AND CONS

Fresh juice, at the very least, is a refreshing treat filled with vitamins, minerals, and vegetable enzymes. The quality of the vitamins is equaled only by eating the whole raw fruits and vegetables themselves. All other sources, including cooked fruits and vegetables (fresh cooked, canned, or frozen) and vitamin pills or preparations, process the food sources in some manner. During processing some vitamins are destroyed (different vitamins are affected by different processes, some by heat or light and others by leaching into cooking waters), but the vitamins from juicing are unprocessed and therefore of high quality.

The most obvious advantage of drinking juice is that it energizes you. This surge of energy occurs because juice is metabolized quickly by the body. What you won't get from drinking juice is a cure for any disease that ails you. Certain fruits and vegetables are helpful in treating some ailments but under no circumstances should you treat any serious physical symptoms with juice "therapy" without consulting your physician. If you believe in the healing powers of juices, use them in conjunction with sound medical advice.

A few words of caution about drinking fruit juices: As mentioned, they are metabolized very quickly. Fruit juice provides a lot of sugar (fructose—a natural sugar) very quickly. If you are diabetic, check with your doctor before indulging in straight fruit juice.

A final warning is to beware of too much of a good thing. In juicing, as in most things, if some is good, more is not necessarily better. Unlike water-soluble vitamins, which are excreted when taken in excess, excess fat-soluble vitamins (A, D, E, and K) are stored in your body. This leads to the possibility of overdoses. For example, too much carrot juice, which by now we all know is just loaded with beta carotene (pre-vitamin A), may turn your skin orange. That's a sure sign that you've overdosed. When you cut back on the carrot juice your skin will return to its normal color, but the healthier way to avoid overdoses is to be moderate in your consumption in the first place. Drink a variety of different juices each day and that way you will get some of everything (a good thing) and not too much of any one nutrient.

What Machine Is Right for You?

There is no one juice machine that is perfect for everyone. The best machine for you depends on your needs, preferences, and constraints.

5

Here are some features that differ from one machine to the next. Pick the machine with the most features that appeal to you.

Types of Juicers

There are five basic types of juicers available. Blenders also can make some types of juices.

Reamers: These can be manual or electric and are used for citrus juicing. A reamer is a ridged cone that can be attached to a handle for hand-held juicing, attached to a dish also for manual juicing, or attached to an engine for electric juicing. Electric reamers can be found as single-use appliances or as attachments for other electrical appliances such as juice extractors, electric mixers, or kitchen centers.

In general, reamers meant specifically for lemons and limes are smaller than those for oranges and grapefruits. Citrus fruits are cut in half, then placed on top of the reamer for juicing. In general, reamers do a better job of juicing citrus fruits (and require less preparation) than centrifugal juice extractors.

Centrifugal Juicers: With these machines, vegetables and fruits are fed into a very fine shredding blade encased in a fine mesh basket, which is spinning at a great speed. The vegetables get shredded, then the pulp gets spun into a container for disposal. The juice is separated and drains into a glass or catcher placed under a spout. This is the most common type of juicer and the type I've tested. The effectiveness and performance of these machines vary, depending on the power of the motor and on engineering designs.

Masticating Juicers: As the name implies, these machines chew up the fruits and vegetables and separate the juice from the pulp. Fruits and vegetables are fed to a cutter that has rows of sharp teeth that grind the produce into a pulp. There is a fine sieve or mesh under the cutter that allows the juice to fall into a container below it and the pulp is then expelled through a separate opening. In addition to making juice, these masticators can also grind, grate, homogenize (make nut butters from shelled nuts, or sorbet from frozen juice), and can juice wheat grass. They tend to be quite large and, in general, more costly than centrifugal juicers.

The most commonly available masticating juicer is the Champion ($249). It's a large machine (21 inches long by 8 inches wide) with an incredibly powerful motor. It comes with a strainer, a funnel for ease of adding small items such as blueberries, and a very good instruction manual. It has continual disposal, and you can fasten a plastic bag to the machine (using a rubber band) so there is no equipment to clean from the pulp disposal. This machine works more slowly than centrifugal extractors and produces a slightly pulpy juice. Cleaning and assembly are both more complicated than with the centrifugal machines.

Hydraulic Presses: These machines work like wine presses. They are quite large and expensive. Only the most serious juice enthusiasts need even consider these machines.

Slow-Turning Juicers: These machines are intended to juice wheat grass—an entire subject by itself. There are books devoted entirely to this subject for anyone seeking more information on these juicers and wheat grass juice.

Blenders: These are not technically juicers, since juicers separate most or all of the pulp from the juice. But blender juices have some advantages over other juices in that they retain all the nutrients (including fiber) of the whole fruit. On the other hand, most blenders are not capable of pulverizing hard fruits or vegetables. Soft fruits such as berries and bananas can be combined with some liquid and made into a beverage in a blender. Blender drinks that combine dairy products with fruits have the added plus of protein. You will find a few blender recipes in this book.

One blender that is promoted as a juicer is Vita-Mix. It's a blender with an ultra-strong motor that can reverse its blade direction, allowing for an incredible ability to pulverize. This machine can juice hard and soft fruits and vegetables, but it doesn't separate the pulp from the juice. The result is a very pulpy beverage that in some instances

7

requires liquid to thin it out. The juice from the Vita-Mix has the nutritional benefits of blender juice, but doesn't have the same smoothness of a true juice.

Cost

For some people this is the most important factor in choosing a juicer. Juicers range in price from $29 to over $1,000, with a wide variety in between. All of them make juice; some do so more efficiently than others.

When shopping for appliances, attempt to accurately predict how long you will use that machine. If you are a gadget addict (like me), and must have the latest machine (which will end up in the closet with your bread, pasta, and ice cream makers), a moderately priced juicer is perfectly satisfactory and will certainly perform long and well enough before finding its permanent home in your closet or at your garage sale.

If you are the type of person with real follow through, or if you will be juicing large quantities at a time, higher priced machines have stronger motors than lower priced ones and may be worth the invest-ment.

Safety Locks

If you have young children, this should be the most important factor in your choice of juicer. Some machines have double safety catches so that it is virtually impossible for a child to remove the lid while the blade is rotating. Others will operate even with the top open.

Ease of Assembly

Although all machines may be easy to clean, assembly and disassembly may be considerably different from one machine to the next. Make sure you can perform this crucial task easily.

Ease of Cleaning

All juice machines are easy to clean if you clean them the instant you finish juicing (which is a good habit to develop). In fact, all you have to do is rinse the parts under warm running water and the machine is ready to use again (except the strainer, which will require a little brushing). On the other hand, if you forget to wash the parts and the pulp dries onto the machine, then you're looking at a big cleanup job.

I determined ease of cleaning by both the number of parts and the number of nooks and crannies in each part.

9

Efficiency

Some machines extract more juice from the fruits and vegetables than others. There is also the consideration of how the machine accomplishes the task—does it shake, rattle, and roll when you put in a carrot, or does it purr? Does the plunger ease in and out or does it get stuck and require Hercules to finish the job?

Capacity

If you are planning to make one glass of juice at a time for just yourself or for two people, any juicer will be able to do the job. If, on the other hand, you plan to make juice for a lot of people at once, then capacity becomes important.

How much juice you can make is limited by three factors: (1) how much pulp the machine can hold; (2) how much juice the catcher can hold; and (3) how long the engine will continue without stalling or burning out.

Juicers that expel the pulp, instead of collecting it in a chamber of the machine, can make almost unlimited amounts without stopping to clean out the machine. Some machines offer a compromise: they have built-in pulp collectors that can be removed from the machine without removing the top or other parts. When your machine reaches its pulp collecting capacity it may begin to whine or shake. Stop the machine and empty the pulp collector before continuing to juice.

Some machines have built-in catchers, which collect the juice. Other machines have a spout that pours into a glass placed under it. If your machine requires you to furnish the glass, it means that there is one less piece of the machine to wash, since you will be using a glass to drink out of anyway. On the other hand, I have been known to forget to put a glass under the spout and have ended up with spinach juice all over my counter and floor. I have found, in some models, that if the glass you place under the spout is not tall enough, the juice will splash as it drops into the glass, which is especially unwelcome when your shirt is white and your juice is purple. Of course you can avoid this problem by using a tall glass. The juicers that have catchers eliminate the possibility of splashing (and forgetting).

Many machines suggest that you limit the amount of time you let the motor run. A suggested running time and resting time is generally given in the instruction booklet that comes with your juicer.

Footprint or Size

One way to encourage use of your juicer is to keep it within convenient reach. This usually means keeping it on the kitchen counter. If your kitchen has only a small amount of counter space, the footprint, or amount of space that a juicer takes up, may be a primary factor in choosing which one is best for you.

Chute Size

The amount of preparation you will have to perform depends partly on the size and shape of the chute. The smaller the chute, the smaller you must cut the produce to fit through it. Half-moon, oval, and rectangular chutes accommodate larger pieces than do kidney shapes.

11

ACME • *Supreme Juicerator*

RETAIL PRICE $259

FOOTPRINT: 9-inch circle

CHUTE SIZE: 1¾ x 1-inch rectangle

BUILT-IN GLASS: No

PULP DISPOSAL: Pulp remains in unit; must stop machine and open to remove pulp. Because the Acme juices so efficiently, there is very little pulp remaining. Exact pulp capacity is hard to judge.

ASSEMBLY AND CLEANING: Top twists on to attach. Blade is not part of strainer basket, but is attached to basket with a large screw knob. The strainer basket is difficult to wash due to a U-shaped lip on the basket, which prevents the pulp from rinsing through.

NUMBER OF PARTS TO CLEAN: 6

SAFETY FEATURES: While the twist-off top requires some strength and manual dexterity, you can, unfortunately, twist off the top long before the basket stops spinning.

USE: The motor is strong and juices smoothly with little effort required. When strainer is full (which happened after just 1 pound of carrots) the machine screeches and vibrates and even moves. This does not stop immediately upon turning off the machine, but continues on for about a minute.

THE JUICE: This machine juices most efficiently of all. It produces the greatest amount of juice from a given amount of produce (Acme produced almost 1 cup of tomato juice from an 8-ounce tomato, whereas most other juicers produced between ½ and ⅔ cup). The juice tends to be thicker than that from other juicers as well.

EXTRA FEATURES: Filters, which remove any pulp from the juice, are available (about $10 for 200) to help ease the cleanup job.

Citrus juicer attachment is available, but was not tested.

COMMENTS: This machine operates slightly differently from most others. The motor is very strong and it takes a minute or two before the basket stops spinning.

BRAUN • *Deluxe Juice Extractor MP 80*

RETAIL PRICE: $90

FOOTPRINT: 9½ x 6½-inch oval

CHUTE SIZE: 2½ x 1⅛-inch kidney shape

BUILT-IN GLASS: No

PULP DISPOSAL: 6-cup capacity—built-in container that can be removed for emptying without opening the rest of machine.

ASSEMBLY AND CLEANING: Cleaning is not especially difficult; assembly tends to be slightly more complicated than most.

NUMBER OF PARTS TO CLEAN: 5 (plus optional pieces)

SAFETY FEATURES: Very good. Must press buttons on either side to release top, and machine cannot be opened unless motor is off.

USE: Requires very little pressure to press produce into the strainer; the motor seems quite strong.

THE JUICE: Produces average amounts of juice, but the juice is slightly pulpier than most.

EXTRA FEATURES: Fruit tray for berries and other small pieces; cup with optional compartment for removing foam from juice; pulp strainer that fits into pulp catcher and allows drainage and collection of extra juice (not of significance when juicing small amounts); cord storage compartment.

13

COMMENTS: Clearly this was a well-thought-out and engineered machine; unfortunately, it has a confusing instruction manual.

TRILLIUM • *Juiceman Jr.*

RETAIL PRICE: $149

FOOTPRINT: 11 x 7-inch rectangle, including pulp disposal container

CHUTE SIZE: 2¼ x 1-inch kidney shape

BUILT-IN GLASS: No

PULP DISPOSAL: Continuous disposal (separate pulp container supplied: 11-cup capacity).

ASSEMBLY AND CLEANING: Fairly easy assembly. Pulp that has not fallen into the disposal container remains in the top and care must be taken when disassembling the machine so that it doesn't fall onto the counter.

NUMBER OF PARTS TO CLEAN: 5

SAFETY FEATURES: Very good. On/off switch is located under latches that hold top onto machine. When in the on position, it is so close to the latch that you must turn the switch off in order to fit finger under latch to release.

USE: Easy to use. Doesn't require excessive pressure to juice hard vegetables.

THE JUICE: Produces average amounts of well-strained juice.

EXTRA FEATURES: Comes with audio cassette of instructions for operation, as well as black and white instruction booklet with some nutrition information and recipes.

COMMENTS: Available in retail outlets. If you don't place the pulp catcher correctly you will end up with a messy counter (and maybe wall).

TRILLIUM • *Juiceman* II

RETAIL PRICE: $289

FOOTPRINT: 9½ x 6½-inch rectangle, including separate pulp disposal unit

CHUTE SIZE: 2½ x 1¼-inch kidney shape

BUILT-IN GLASS: No

PULP DISPOSAL: Continuous pulp disposal (separate pulp container supplied: 12-cup capacity).

ASSEMBLY AND CLEANING: The assembly is somewhat complicated, with parts requiring rotating and assembling in a given order; when disassembling, the top must be rotated completely or blade will not release. Parts clean easily, but bottom of chute accumulates pulp and care must be taken when disassembling the top that the pulp doesn't drop onto the counter.

15

NUMBER OF PARTS TO CLEAN: 5

SAFETY FEATURES: Very good. Top twists on and will not release until on/off switch is in off position.

USE: This machine is quieter than most and handles all jobs with ease.

THE JUICE: Produces an average amount of juice that is not too pulpy.

EXTRA FEATURES: Comes with a video cassette that gives very clear (and necessary) instructions on assembly and use. If you do not have a VHS player, there is also an instructional and recipe booklet.

COMMENTS: A good machine. However, if you don't place the pulp catcher in just the right position, you can have a mess on your counter. Available through direct mail. 1-800-800-8455.

16

KRUPS • *VitaMight Model 294*

RETAIL PRICE: $40

FOOTPRINTS: 9½ x 5½-inch oval

CHUTE SIZE: 2 x 1-inch kidney shape

BUILT-IN GLASS: No

PULP DISPOSAL: Interior pulp disposal requires disassembling machine. 4-cup capacity.

ASSEMBLY AND CLEANING: Has fairly elaborate, though not too difficult, assembly mechanisms. Cleaning is no harder than average.

NUMBER OF PARTS TO CLEAN: 3 (4 if you are using optional juice catcher)

SAFETY FEATURES: Fairly good. You must turn the switch from the on position to the unlock position before you can remove top; however, you can do this quickly enough so that the blade may still be rotating when you lift the top.

USE: When juicing carrots, there was some occasional shaking and movement and a fair amount of hesitation that required tamping the carrots with the pusher to encourage the machine to continue.

THE JUICE: The juice is not too pulpy, but the amount produced is just slightly less than average.

EXTRA FEATURES: Provides a cup to catch the juice.

COMMENTS: Not a very heavy-duty extractor, but it performed adequately with the less hard fruits and vegetables. The spout is quite close to the body of the machine, so if you choose to use a drinking glass to catch the juice (instead of the plastic container provided), make sure that it is not too low and can fit close to the machine or the juice will slop down the side of the machine. Instruction booklet not clear.

17

MOULINEX • *Deluxe Juice Extractor Model* 753

RETAIL PRICE: $80

FOOTPRINT: 9½ x 7-inch oval

CHUTE SIZE: 2½ x 1¼-inch kidney shape

BUILT-IN GLASS: No

PULP DISPOSAL: Built-in pulp catcher has a handle that makes it easy to empty without opening the machine. 5½-cup capacity.

ASSEMBLY AND CLEANING: Machine is easy to assemble as long as you remember to do it before sliding in the pulp catcher. Cleaning is no harder than average, although there are a fair number of nooks and crannies under the lid.

NUMBER OF PARTS TO CLEAN: 5

SAFETY FEATURES: Very good. On/off switch is located under the latches that hold the top to the machine, and the space under the latch is too small to fit your fingers into unless you first turn the switch to the off position.

USE: Easy to work. Motor feels substantial. Some slight hesitation when juicing carrots.

THE JUICE: Produces an average amount of not too pulpy juice.

EXTRA FEATURES: Cord storage built into machine.

COMMENTS: This machine is very similar in design to the Juiceman Jr., with the main exception that the pulp disposal unit is built in. Moulinex sent a nicely designed second model that was smaller than this and about half the price, but, unfortunately, it died halfway into the first test. I was assured by a company representative that it will send a new model to customers who have similar problems with their juicers.

OSTER • *3.23-08*

RETAIL PRICE: $80

FOOTPRINT: 10 x 7-inch rectangle

CHUTE SIZE: 2¼ x 1-inch kidney shape

BUILT-IN GLASS: No

PULP DISPOSAL: Large built-in pulp catcher with finger holds for easy removal without having to open machine. 7-cup capacity.

ASSEMBLY AND CLEANING: Fairly easy to assemble as long as you slide pulp catcher into place after assembly. Depth of hood makes cleaning a little awkward.

NUMBER OF PARTS TO CLEAN: 5

SAFETY FEATURES: Poor. Can open and remove top while motor is still running.

Use: Moderately noisy, but no hesitation during operation.

The juice: Makes a slightly better than average amount of juice with no noticeable pulp.

Extra features: Has two speeds: high for hard fruits and vegetables and low for soft. Provides a brush for cleaning out strainer. Good instruction book with some recipes.

Comments: This is a fairly large machine and the spout is a little too close to the machine, so it's best to find a glass that fits close to the machine to prevent splattering.

PERFECT JUICER • *Model MJ600*

Retail price: $69.95

Footprint: 11 x 6-inch rectangle

Chute size: 2¼ x 1⅛-inch football shape. This shape can accommodate fairly large round pieces (such as carrots) without having to trim them further.

Built-in glass: No

Pulp disposal: Built-in pulp container with a plastic liner that can be lifted out. However, you have to remove lid to empty it. 3½-cup capacity.

ASSEMBLY AND CLEANING: Moderately easy to assemble and clean although there are some nooks and crannies that are hard to get to and the latches are sometimes hard to open.

NUMBER OF PARTS TO CLEAN: 5

SAFETY FEATURES: Poor. You can unlatch and remove top while the motor is still running.

USE: Fairly noisy to operate, with some hesitation while juicing carrots.

THE JUICE: Produces a slightly above average amount of juice that is not too pulpy. However, the machine imparts a plastic flavor to juices that have a mild flavor. This might happen only when the machine is new.

EXTRA FEATURES: Has two speeds: high for hard fruits and vegetables and low for soft ones. Includes a brush to clean strainer mesh and a small spatula.

COMMENTS: The head of the plunger is smaller than most and less comfortable to grip.

PHOENIX • *ESG 103*

RETAIL PRICE: $169.95

FOOTPRINT: 11 x 6-inch oval

CHUTE SIZE: 2½ x 1⅛-inch kidney shape

BUILT-IN GLASS: No

PULP DISPOSAL: Has a pulp container with a hand grip that can be emptied without opening the machine. 10-cup capacity.

ASSEMBLY AND CLEANING: Relatively easy to assemble and clean.

NUMBER OF PARTS TO CLEAN: 5

SAFETY FEATURES: Good. Cannot unlatch top unless switch is in off position.

USE: A good strong motor. This machine feels well constructed, although there was some hesitation while juicing carrots. Some pulp may back up into chute and make the plunger stick a little.

THE JUICE: Makes slightly more than the average amount of juice; not too much pulp.

EXTRA FEATURES: Has two speeds: high for hard fruits and vegetables and low for soft.

COMMENTS: A nice machine, a little on the large side.

SALTON • *Vitamin Bar—Model JC3*

RETAIL PRICE: $85

FOOTPRINT: 8 x 5-inch oval

CHUTE SIZE: 1½ x 1-inch U shape

BUILT-IN GLASS: No

PULP DISPOSAL: Built-in pulp collector; must open machine to empty. 4-cup capacity.

ASSEMBLY AND CLEANING: Easier to take apart than put together. Pulp container is narrow to reach into to clean, otherwise not too difficult to clean.

NUMBER OF PARTS TO CLEAN: 4 (5 if using juice catcher)

SAFETY FEATURES: Good. Must turn off machine to disengage top.

USE: The machine was moderately noisy, but did not hesitate when juicing.

THE JUICE: Makes slightly less than the average amount of juice that is not too pulpy.

EXTRA FEATURES: Has citrus juice attachment. Provides plastic cup catcher for juice.

COMMENTS: The spout is built close to the body of the machine and if you are not using the plastic cup provided, the glass you use must fit the machine well or the juice will splatter over the machine and counter. Salton sent two of the same model for testing: one was slightly quieter than the other but had a temperamental on/off switch that had to be turned to the "on" position numerous times before the motor would start; at other times it would start on the first try. The second machine had no problem starting, but was noisier than the first.

SANYO • *Julius Plus Model #SJ3100BW*

RETAIL PRICE: $104

FOOTPRINT: 8 x 7-inch rectangle

CHUTE SIZE: 2 x 1½-inch half-moon

BUILT-IN GLASS: Yes

PULP DISPOSAL: Must open machine to clean out pulp. It did reach its capacity with the 1½-pound carrot test. Capacity size is hard to measure but is guesstimated at 3 to 3½ cups.

ASSEMBLY AND CLEANING: Relatively easy to clean and assemble.

NUMBER OF PARTS TO CLEAN: 6

SAFETY FEATURES: Poor. You can operate this machine without the top while the motor is running.

USE: The machine hesitates occasionally and requires some tamping with the plunger to help foods along.

THE JUICE: A slightly higher than average amount of not too pulpy juice.

EXTRA FEATURES: This machine can be a blender as well as an extractor. It also shaves ice cubes into sherbet and has a whipping attachment for egg whites, whipped cream, and milkshakes. It has an on/off/pulse option, although the pulse is really for the blender attachment. It also comes with a brush for the strainer.

COMMENTS: The half-moon shape of the chute accommodates large pieces of fruits and vegetables. I bought this machine about five years ago because I needed a new blender and thought it was a good value to get the juicer attachment essentially free. I remember being perfectly satisfied with the way the juicer worked when I bought it, even though it doesn't operate especially well compared to the other machines. There are two possible reasons for this: (1) ignorance is bliss, or (2) the machine worked better when it was new. I asked Sanyo if it wanted to submit a new machine for my testing, since it would be compared to all other new machines, and Sanyo said it would stand on the result from my old one.

SINGER • *Juice Giant*

25

RETAIL PRICE: $59.95

FOOTPRINT: 8½ x 6½-inch rectangle

CHUTE SIZE: 2 x ⅞-inch kidney shape

BUILT-IN GLASS: Yes

PULP DISPOSAL: Built-in catcher that can be removed for disposal without opening the machine. 3-cup capacity.

ASSEMBLY AND CLEANING: Assembly is not hard as long as you line up the juice and pulp containers correctly. Lots of nooks and crannies in the top that need rinsing.

NUMBER OF PARTS TO CLEAN: 6

SAFETY FEATURES: Good. Motor automatically stops when the latches are opened.

USE: Moderately noisy, with some hesitation toward the end of the carrot testing.

THE JUICE: Produces average amounts of juice. Not too much pulp.

EXTRA FEATURES: Good instruction booklet.

COMMENTS: Although the capacity of the pulp catcher is small, it is easy to empty.

26 TEFAL • *Juice Master*

RETAIL PRICE: $99.99

FOOTPRINT: 8-inch round

CHUTE SIZE: 2⅛ x 1-inch half-moon or kidney shape

BUILT-IN GLASS: No

PULP DISPOSAL: Must open machine and disassemble to clean. 4-cup capacity.

ASSEMBLY AND CLEANING: Assembly fairly easy, with not too many parts to clean. However, pulp container is deep and narrow and hard to fit hand into, when necessary.

Number of parts to clean: 4

Safety features: Very good. Top must be twisted into position for the machine to start (like the old Cuisinart), then must be untwisted to stop motor. Release button must be pressed to take top off.

Use: This machine gets noisy and shakes toward the end of the juicing process. Although the safety features are excellent, it does require some strength to turn the top into proper position for operating, especially if your hands are wet.

The juice: Makes slightly less than average amount with not too much pulp.

Extra features: Citrus juicer, which works very well.

Comments: This machine tends to send the juice splashing if you do not use a tall glass that fits just under the spout. It is a little more awkward to operate than the machines that have on/off switches.

27

A Shopper's Guide to Fruits and Vegetables

In the bad old days, when supermarkets used to stock only the worst looking and most uninteresting produce, I always wondered who would buy it. The answer is: my father. Whenever he's sent out to pick up a few items, you can be sure that he'll come back with the saddest produce around. The point to this story is that for juicing, as for most things, what goes in, comes out. If you put in underripe, flavorless fruit, you're going to make flavorless juice. It's important, then, to know how to pick good fruits and vegetables.

As I've been writing this section about choosing fruits and vegetables, it became apparent to me that this is a project I've been preparing for most of my adult life. Unlike some people who prefer to do all their food shopping for the week, or longer, at one time; I love to shop for food daily, buying only what is ripe that day. Of course, living in New York City where there are fruit stands on almost every corner, this is not a hard, or even an unusual, thing to do. On my way home from work, I just stop and shop and find this relaxing. Consequently, I've been studying produce shopping for many a year.

My quickest, easiest rule of thumb (for those of you who don't want to read about each item individually) is that vegetables should be hard and not have soft spots, which indicate bruises. Fruits should be soft (not mushy, but just give a little when gently squeezed), smell fragrant when sniffed (if you can't smell it, it probably isn't at its flavor peak), and never have wrinkles. Both fruits and vegetables should have naturally shiny skin (that's why markets oil some produce—to make it appear shiny).

The exceptions to these rules are:

APPLES should definitely be hard.

AVOCADOS should give when pressed, like ripe fruit.

LEAFY VEGETABLES should not be brown at the edges, nor should they be wilted.

MELONS are usually hard, but will give a little when pressed on the blossom end.

SUMMER SQUASH (zucchini and yellow squash), cucumbers, and eggplant should not be rock hard, nor should they be as soft as ripe fruit, but rather somewhere in between.

TOMATOES should give when pressed, like ripe fruit.

WHAT ABOUT ORGANIC FRUITS AND VEGETABLES?

Organic vegetables are grown with a minimum of pesticides and other unhealthy compounds. This is a major advantage, since rinsing or even peeling fruits and vegetables doesn't ensure that you have removed all potentially harmful substances. The best way to do that is to buy organic.

The down side of organic produce is that it's more expensive and is cosmetically less perfect. By eliminating pesticides entirely or switching to safer (and more expensive) but possibly less effective pesticides (i.e., natural ones), the organic farmer will lose more crops to pests and will also have more damaged goods. These costs are passed along to consumers.

31

ABOUT THE SHOPPING GUIDE

Season: Due to the greatly improved methods of transportation, many fruits and vegetables that were strictly seasonal have become available almost all year. And those that are not may now have two seasons instead of one: the local season and a second season when the produce is imported from South America, Australia, New Zealand, or Africa. Local produce is usually lower in cost and can be tree or vine ripened because it doesn't get shipped. It also requires less storage time, and therefore has a better nutrient profile. Very little, if any, imported produce is organically grown and, further, some countries allow growers to use pesticides that we have banned.

Preparation: My advice about preparing fruits and vegetables for juicing is, if you wouldn't eat it—don't juice it.

Bruised and inedible parts of fruits and vegetables are frequently bitter or, at least, less sweet than the edible portions of the produce. Although the juicer will spin out rind, seeds, and other inedible pieces, some of the bitterness will likely be imparted to the juice. Rather than risk an unpleasant juice, just discard the inedible parts before juicing.

Further, I use the pulp for cooking or for snacks. In the leftovers section ("Waste Not, Want Not," pages 153–63) I offer suggestions for the pulp. Including the rind and seeds makes the pulp useless for anything other than the garbage or mulch pile.

The juice: I've tried to give an idea of the amount and type of juice you get from any given fruit or vegetable. This will help you choose combinations and quantities.

Nutrition: Nutritional information for fruits and vegetables is sometimes inconsistent because the nutrients in the same fruit or vegetable vary, determined by the composition of soil, weather conditions, variety of the fruit or vegetable (Granny Smith, Crispin, and Northern Spy apples, for example), length and conditions of storage, and, finally, processing. Heat and light both degrade the nutrient content of foods. Canned and bottled juices have all been processed by pasteurization, concentration, or freeze drying and have a poorer nutrient profile than freshly picked or juiced fruits and vegetables.

The nutrition information given in the produce alphabet is for the serving size of the whole fruit or vegetable described (not for the juice). The percentages of nutrients discussed below are for the Rec-

ommended Dietary Allowances (RDA) published by the National
Research Council. The following are the RDA for adults:

AGES 25–50

	MALE	FEMALE
Vitamin A	1,000 RE *	800 RE *
Vitamin C	60.0 mg	60.0 mg
Thiamin (B$_1$)	1.5 mg	1.1 mg
Riboflavin (B$_2$)	1.7 mg	1.3 mg
Niacin (B$_3$)	20.0 mg	15.0 mg
Calcium	800.0 mg	800.0 mg
Iron	10.0 mg	15.0 mg

* RE = retinol equivalent.

Figures for juice are not available for most produce. I sent samples
of some fruit and vegetable juices to be analyzed to ascertain whether
fresh juice is really as nutrient packed as we have been led to believe.
The results bear out the fact that what goes in comes out. Apples, for
instance, which do not have an impressive profile, yield a juice that
is not too impressive either. Spinach and carrots, on the other hand,
are both rich in vitamins and minerals.

Since nutrient quality will vary from one glass of juice to the next,
for reasons stated earlier, these figures should be used as guidelines,
not gospel. This is especially obvious when you look at the vitamin A
(actually beta carotene) content of the carrot juice. The figures are

high—so high that the laboratory called to ask what I had added to the juice. In fact, I just juiced a seemingly normal bunch of carrots that turned out to be nutrition dynamos. The USDA figures for the total amount of vitamin A in the 14 ounces of carrots required to make a 6-ounce glass of juice is 11,162 RE. Even if all the vitamin A in the carrot goes into the juice and none remains in the pulp (which I doubt is the case), that is still less than the 13,898 RE reported in the juice analyzed.

The following tables show the results of the juices that I had analyzed. All figures are for 6 ounces of juice.

Carrot Juice

	ABSOLUTE #	% RDA MALE	% RDA FEMALE
Calories	62		
Carbohydrates	12 g		
Vitamin A	13,898 RE *	1,389	1,737
Vitamin C	17.0 mg	28	28
Thiamin (B_1)	.07 mg	5	6
Riboflavin (B_2)	.12 mg	7	9
Niacin (B_3)	2.14 mg	11	14
Potassium	533.0 mg	**	**
Calcium	24.0 mg	2	2
Iron	.9 mg	8	6

* RE = retinol equivalent.
** Exact requirement not established; 1,600 mg to 2,000 mg is an acceptable range.

35

Spinach Juice

	ABSOLUTE #	% RDA MALE	% RDA FEMALE
Calories	56		
Carbohydrates	1 g		
Vitamin A	1,000 RE *	100	125
Vitamin C	11 mg	18	18
Thiamin (B$_1$)	.08 mg	5	7
Riboflavin (B$_2$)	.25 mg	15	19
Niacin (B$_3$)	.59 mg	3	4
Potassium	700 mg	**	**
Calcium	35 mg	3	3
Iron	4.01 mg	33	27

* RE = retinol equivalent.
** Exact requirement not established; 1,600 mg to 2,000 mg is an acceptable range.

Tomato Juice

	ABSOLUTE #	% RDA MALE	% RDA FEMALE
Calories	19		
Carbohydrates	3 g		
Vitamin A	145 RE *	15	18
Vitamin C	20 mg	33	33
Thiamin (B$_1$)	.05 mg	3	5
Riboflavin (B$_2$)	.05 mg	3	4
Niacin (B$_3$)	1.02 mg	5	7
Potassium	330 mg	**	**
Calcium	8 mg	0	0
Iron	.82 mg	7	5

* RE = retinol equivalent.
** Exact requirement not established; 1,600 mg to 2,000 mg is an acceptable range.

Apple Juice

	ABSOLUTE #	% RDA MALE	% RDA FEMALE
Calories	76		
Carbohydrates	18 g		
Vitamin A	0	0	0
Vitamin C	5 mg	7	7
Thiamin (B₁)	.02 mg	1	2
Riboflavin (B₂)	.05 mg	3	4
Niacin (B₃)	.02 mg	1	1
Potassium	85 mg	*	*
Calcium	7 mg	0	0
Iron	.45 mg	4	3

* Exact requirement not established; 1,600 mg to 2,000 mg is an acceptable range.

Cantaloupe Juice

	ABSOLUTE #	% RDA MALE	% RDA FEMALE
Calories	62		
Carbohydrates	14 g		
Vitamin A	1,521 RE *	150	190
Vitamin C	60 mg	100	100
Thiamin (B$_1$)	.03 mg	2	3
Riboflavin (B$_2$)	.07 mg	4	5
Niacin (B$_3$)	1.14 mg	6	8
Potassium	440 mg	**	**
Calcium	12.0 mg	1	1
Iron	.71 mg	6	5

* RE = retinol equivalent.
** Exact requirement not established; 1,600 mg to 2,000 mg is an acceptable range.

Strawberry Juice

	ABSOLUTE #	% RDA MALE	% RDA FEMALE
Calories	57		
Carbohydrates	10 g		
Vitamin A	0	0	0
Vitamin C	119 mg	200	200
Thiamin (B_1)	.05 mg	3	5
Riboflavin (B_2)	.12 mg	7	9
Niacin (B_3)	.87 mg	4	6
Potassium	210 mg	**	**
Calcium	10 mg	1	1
Iron	.79 mg	7	5

** Exact requirement not established; 1,600 mg to 2,000 mg is an acceptable range.

RIPENING

Although you should try to buy each piece of produce at its peak of perfection, this is not always possible. Vegetables (except tomatoes and avocados) come to market fully ripe and the only problem is that they may be overripe or spoiled. Fruits frequently come to market underripe. Most can be ripened after purchasing.

Fruits that are slightly underripe can be easily ripened at room temperature in a day or two. Ripening can be hastened slightly by placing the fruit on a windowsill or in a paper bag. Fruits that are extremely underripe will frequently start to rot before becoming fully ripe, or they may soften without becoming more flavorful or juicy. One way to prevent ripening fruits from rotting in spots is to rotate them daily, rather than letting them stand on one side during the entire ripening. Once fruits have reached desired ripeness, refrigerate to prevent overripening.

Berries do not ripen after picking. Leaving them at room temperature will only hasten their deterioration.

A PRODUCE ALPHABET

Apples
Apples come in hundreds or even thousands of varieties, many only regionally available. Local apples, in season, are usually fresh and at their peak. Any type of apple is suitable for juicing, even baking varieties, which tend to have a mealy texture when eaten raw.

Most varieties of apples are slightly or very tart. The only truly sweet apples nationally available are the red or Golden Delicious. I use apples in these recipes primarily to sweeten other fruits or vegetables, therefore I usually call for Delicious apples by name.

Serving size: 1 medium apple (about 4½ ounces)

Nutrition: One 4-ounce apple is 72 calories. Although apples are excellent sources of fiber when eaten whole, they contain only modest amounts of most nutrients. One apple contains less than 5 percent of the RDA for everything except vitamin C, of which it contains 8 percent (nothing to brag about compared to the orange or other high C fruits).

Season: September to June, depending on the variety

Shopping: Look for apples that have a natural shine to the skin. Avoid bruise marks, punctures, cuts, and abrasions. When pressed gently, apples should feel hard; there should be no give. Softness or wrinkling indicates apples well beyond their prime.

Preparation: Rinse thoroughly; discard stem and seeds (it's important to discard apple seeds because they contain a minute quantity of poison). Remember, apples oxidize quickly when exposed to the air, so don't prepare them too far in advance of juicing, and don't let the juice stand too long after making it or it will turn brown.

The juice: 1 medium apple, cored (4½ ounces) yields approximately ⅓ cup of thin, sweet juice. The apple flavor tends to dominate other fruits and vegetables juiced with it.

Apricots

Apricots have a short season and are very perishable, which means enjoy them when you can get them. They do not ripen well off the vine, therefore should be bought ripe and eaten soon after. Fully ripe apricots are sweet with a hint of tartness. Underripe apricots can be downright sour.

Serving size: Apricots are small and a serving consists of 2 whole ones (3 ounces).

Nutrition: One serving is 34 calories. Apricots are an excellent source of beta carotene (a serving is 24 percent of the RDA) and a fairly good source of vitamins C and E.

Season: June to July. Imported apricots can be found in December, January, or February.

Shopping: Look for plump apricots, yellow-orange in color, preferably with a pink blush on the cheeks. Avoid apricots that are pale and/or green at the top (around the stem). The skin should have a velvety feel; the fruit should not be too soft (as that indicates a mushy, not ripe, fruit) and feel heavy for the size.

Preparation: Rinse thoroughly. Cut in half and remove pit.

The juice: You get about 1 tablespoon of juice per ounce of apricot. It's one of the soft fruits that produce more of a purée than a juice, and therefore the juice tends to stay in the well of the extractor and needs a thin juice to wash it through into the glass. Depending upon the ripeness of the fruit, apricot juice varies from very to slightly tart.

43

Asparagus

Asparagus are available pretty much all year, not just in the spring. Although they are usually eaten cooked, they are perfectly delicious raw.

Serving size: 6 medium stalks (3 ounces)

Nutrition: Asparagus are a good source of vitamin C (46 percent of the RDA), and fairly good for folacin and vitamin E (21 percent and 22 percent respectively).

Season: March to May

Shopping: Asparagus come in a wide range of thicknesses, and thin or thick is strictly a matter of taste. Fresh asparagus should have tightly closed purple heads, be firm, and never bend or be shriveled. The stalk should have a slight sheen, although the head has a more matte finish. Some green asparagus are white on the bottom; these are okay to buy, but the white part should be snapped off by holding the bottom in both hands and bending. The stalk will naturally snap or break where the tough part begins.

Preparation: Rinse the asparagus thoroughly, snap, and discard any white end of stalk. For eating, part or all of the stalk may be peeled; this is not necessary for juicing.

The juice: 4 medium asparagus (2 ounces) produce 3 tablespoons of slightly pulpy, fairly bitter, fairly thin juice. Because the flavor is quite strong, I recommend pairing asparagus with a large amount of a neutral flavored vegetable such as cucumber.

Avocados

Avocados are grown primarily in Florida and California. The Hass variety (the small ones with the dark nubbly skin) is the most flavorful. Ripe avocados will give slightly when gently pressed. Because of the softness of the flesh, avocados, like bananas, are puréed by the extractor, rather than juiced. Although you can rinse the avocado through with a thin juice, its delicate flavor gets lost. This, coupled with the avocado's high fat content, makes it unsuitable for juicing.

Bananas

Bananas are suitable for juice extractors in small quantities and are fine for blender drinks. They act as sweeteners and thickeners. But bananas should be juiced before adding other fruits and vegetables so the purée will be washed through.

45

For a special treat, I slice peeled ripe bananas into bite-size pieces and freeze them. They make great snacks or can be thrown into the blender with some milk, fresh fruit, juice, or yogurt to make thick shakes.

Serving size: 1 medium banana, peeled (4 ounces)

Nutrition: 1 banana is fairly caloric (105) compared to most other fruits, but it has an impressive profile. It provides 33 percent of the requirement of vitamin B_6 (pyridoxine), 17 percent of vitamin C, 12 percent of potassium, and 11 percent of magnesium, along with smaller amounts of other nutrients.

Season: Year-round

Shopping: You can buy bananas when they are green, yellow, or yellow with brown speckles. When bananas are green, they are underripe and starchy. As they ripen, the starch turns to sugar. Allow bananas to ripen at room temperature until all the green has disappeared (even on the stem). If you wait until the bananas develop some brown speckles, they will be very sweet. Large dark patches on the skin, however, do not indicate ripeness but rather are bruises and these bananas should be avoided. If your bananas are very speckled and you are not ready to use them, they can be refrigerated to prolong their usability. The skin will turn very dark brown when refrigerated, but the fruit will remain edible as long as it doesn't turn to mush.

Preparation: Allow to ripen, then peel. Bananas oxidize quickly, so don't prepare them until just before using. Also serve the juice soon after preparing or it, too, will become brown.

The juice: There is very little banana juice that comes out of the juicer but 1 banana, peeled (4 ounces), yields 2 to 3 tablespoons of banana purée, which thickens and sweetens any juice. Juice the banana first and follow it with a fruit or vegetable that produces a thin juice to wash the purée into the glass.

46

Bean Sprouts

Bean sprouts produce quite a bitter juice with an unpleasant flavor.

Beets

Beets have a slightly sweet, but very earthy flavor.

Some health food "experts" caution that beet juice should be drunk only in limited quantities and never alone. It does have a strong flavor, which is much more pleasant in combination with other vegetables or fruits, and so I never drink plain beet juice for that reason.

The deep purple of beet juice will color any juice added to it. I've also heard more than one person worry about internal bleeding after they have consumed beets or beet juice because beets turn the stool dark and leach into the toilet water. But there is no cause for alarm.

Serving size: 1 medium beet (3½ ounces)

Nutrition: 44 calories. They are a pretty good source of folacin (25 percent of the RDA) and fairly good for potassium (10 percent), with lesser amounts of other nutrients. The greens, which are also edible, have a more impressive nutritional profile.

Season: Year-round

Shopping: Beet roots should always be very firm. If they are at all soft, pass them up. Small beets tend to be more tender than larger ones (although this may not be too important when juicing). If the beets come with greens, the tops should be fresh and not wilted or brown around the edges or at all slimy.

Preparation: Discard tops (unless using them for greens) and roots. Rinse thoroughly, using a scrub brush to get rid of any soil that may be clinging to the root.

The juice: 1 medium beet, trimmed (3½ ounces) yields a very dark purple, thin, earthy flavored, slightly sweet juice.

Belgian Endive
Belgian endive is very bitter and not suitable for juicing.

Blackberries
Blackberries are bigger, darker cousins of raspberries, and range in flavor from extremely tart to sweet, depending upon their ripeness.

Serving size: ½ cup (3 ounces)

Nutrition: 44 calories per serving. Blackberries are a good source of vitamin C (30 percent of the RDA) with moderate amounts of folacin, vitamin E, and magnesium.

Season: June to August. Imported blackberries are available in January or February.

Shopping: Blackberries are extremely perishable so check for mold, especially at the bottom of the box. Mold has a strong recognizable aroma, so use your nose to help. Large blackberries are usually sweeter than small ones.

Preparation: Rinse.

The juice: ¾ cup of berries (4 ounces) yields a scant ¼ cup of quite thick, tart juice.

48

Blueberries

Blueberries come in two varieties, cultivated and wild. The cultivated berries, larger than wild, are more widely available. Blueberries are sometimes referred to as huckleberries, but in fact the two are different, with the huckleberries having larger seeds than the blues.

Serving size: ½ cup (3 ounces)

Nutrition: 48 calories per serving. Good source of vitamins C and E (20 percent of RDA each), with some B vitamins.

Season: June to September; imported berries are available in January or February. Blueberries are available year-round frozen, unsweetened.

Shopping: Wild blueberries should be dark and small with a noticeable crown on top. Cultivated blueberries should be firm and dark with a slight bloom (white powdery blush). The larger cultivated blueberries are usually sweeter than the small ones. The berries should be firm, dry to the touch, and unwrinkled. Unlike raspberries and blackberries, which mold quickly, the first sign of spoilage for blueberries is that the berries are wet and soft.

Preparation: Rinse if fresh, defrost if frozen.

The juice: 1 cup (6 ounces) yields ½ cup of fairly thin, dark blue, slightly sweet/slightly tart juice that separates very quickly.

Broccoli

Broccoli has become an inspired nutritional choice. Findings point to the possibility that broccoli may prevent cancer, among other things. Some people peel the stalks, others just discard them completely. I love the crunchy texture of broccoli stalks and add them to any dish that calls for broccoli—I even slice them and eat them raw as crudités.

Serving size: 1 stalk (4 ounces)

Nutrition: 31 calories. A nutrition bonanza, with 176 percent of the RDA for vitamin C, 22 percent of vitamin A; 20 percent of folacin; and 10 percent of potassium, riboflavin (B_2) and magnesium; a not too shabby 9 percent of pyridoxine (B_6), pantothenic acid, and phosphorus; and fair amounts of thiamin (B_1), iron, calcium, and niacin (B_3).

Season: Year-round

Shopping: Broccoli should never be limp, nor should the florets be yellow. Look for broccoli with firm stems and tightly clustered green florets. If there are any leaves, they should be fresh, not limp.

Preparation: Rinse the broccoli and cut into pieces to fit your chute. Use both the florets and the stem.

The juice: 1 stem (stalk and florets: 4 ounces) yields 3 tablespoons of very pulpy, medium thin juice, with a mild flavor. Some machines spin out most of the florets and yield only a thin nonpulpy juice from the stem.

Cabbage

Cabbage comes in many varieties. The most common are regular green or red cabbages, but there is also the savoy, which has crinkled leaves, and Chinese, which grows more like a head of celery and has a more watery consistency—resembling, and frequently confused with, bok choy.

Serving size: 3 ounces

Nutrition: 20 calories. Cabbage is a very good source of vitamin C (67 percent of the RDA) and a fairly good source of folacin (12 percent), as well as lesser amounts of other nutrients.

Season: Year-round

Shopping: Look for compact heads that don't give when squeezed and are heavy for their size. There should be no cuts or dark marks. If the heads have their outer leaves, they should be dark green and firm. If the outer leaves have been peeled off, the leaves should be green with no hint of yellow.

Preparation: Rinse and roll leaves into a compact bundle.

The juice: 6 ounces of cabbage yield a generous ⅓ cup of thin juice with a strong cabbage flavor, which is peppery, but not bitter.

Cantaloupe

Cantaloupe is a sheer delight when it is ripe. It is one of those previously seasonal fruits that is now available pretty much all year.

Serving size: ¼ melon (4½ to 5 ounces)

Nutrition: At 47 calories, cantaloupe is a nutritional bargain. It provides 94 percent of the RDA for vitamin C and 54 percent of vitamin A, both antioxidants that we keep hearing about as an important factor in good health. It's also a fairly good source of potassium (11 percent), folacin (10 percent) and pyridoxine (8 percent).

Season: Peak months are July and August, but available year-round.

Shopping: All melons are a shopping enigma. Try to find heavy ones that give a little when pressed at the blossom end and, most important, that have some aroma when sniffed. You can shake the melon to see if the seeds slosh a little, as this is supposed to be the sign of a ripe melon as well. I also find that if the color under the netting is deep green it seems to indicate a less ripe melon. Fortunately, many markets sell cantaloupe halves. This way you can really choose one that has deep orange flesh, only a thin green rind, and, most important, you will be able to get a good whiff that should guide you to the ripest melons.

Preparation: Discard skin and seeds before juicing.

The juice: ¼ small cantaloupe, seeded and rind removed (4 ounces), yields ⅓ cup of a sweet, thin, but slightly pulpy juice.

51

Carrots

Carrots are good for your eyes because they're very high in vitamin A and previtamin A (better known as beta carotene). In addition to being good for your eyes, beta carotene is the new star on the anti-aging horizon. It has antioxidant qualities that capture free radicals, which are suspected of causing various symptoms of aging, and it may possibly have some anticancer properties.

Serving size: 1 small carrot (2½ ounces)

Nutrition: For a mere 16 calories, 1 carrot has 253 percent of the RDA of vitamin A. There is some vitamin C (11 percent) and minor amounts of other vitamins and minerals.

Season: Year-round

Shopping: Carrots can vary in flavor and texture from very sweet and crispy to slightly bitter and woody. Look for those that have deep color. I believe that large carrots tend to be sweeter than thin ones (although they can also be woodier). Carrots that are green toward the top of the root tend to be less sweet at the top. If you buy carrots with the tops on, you can be sure they are fairly fresh, unless the tops are wilted, or shriveled and dry. Carrots sold without the tops can be stored longer than those with fresh tops. Any topless carrots that have started to sprout new greens or roots are probably well past their prime. Look for carrots that are very firm and crisp.

Preparation: Rinse thoroughly, scrub with a brush (there is no need to peel carrots used for juicing), and trim the top where the stem joined the root.

The juice: 1 large carrot, trimmed (6 ounces), yields ¼ cup thin, sweet, orange-colored juice.

Cauliflower

Cauliflower is in the cruciferous family (along with broccoli, cabbage, and Brussels sprouts), whose possible anticancer properties are being touted. There is a new vegetable becoming available called Romanesco cauliflower. A cross between cauliflower and broccoli, it grows in a head like a cauliflower, but is green in color and the florets are cone shaped. The flavor is closer to cauliflower than broccoli and it can be used interchangeably with cauliflower.

Serving size: 1 cup florets, 4 ounces

Nutrition: 28 calories. An excellent source of vitamin C (135 percent of the RDA), with a significant amount of folacin (19 percent) and pyridoxine (B_6: 13 percent) and potassium (11 percent).

Season: Year-round

Shopping: Ideally, the cauliflower head comes surrounded by its leaves (most of which have been cut). Check the little inner leaves to see that they are green, not yellow, and fresh looking. The head itself should be tightly closed, as any space among or between the florets indicates age. There should be no brown spots on the white florets.

Preparation: Discard leaves and separate head into florets that will fit into your chute; rinse.

The juice: About ¼ small head of cauliflower (florets: 6 ounces) yields a scant ¼ cup of thin juice that has a grassy flavor, neither bitter nor sweet.

53

Celery

Celery gives you a lot to eat for just a few calories. The first word I think of about celery is "crisp," but for some people the word "diet" comes to mind.

Serving size: 1 medium rib (2 ounces)

Nutrition: 9 calories. Celery is not a powerhouse of nutrients (but what can you expect for 9 calories). The most outstanding figure is that it is naturally high in sodium (relatively speaking, that is) at about 48 mg per stalk. This makes it a great choice for those days when you are exercising vigorously and need to replace not just the water your body has lost sweating, but also the salt.

Season: Year-round

Shopping: All celery should be very crisp; if any ribs are wilted, pass it up. If there are outer leaves on the bunch you are considering, they should be fresh, green, and never yellowed (although the leaves on the inner heart will be much more yellow). Outer ribs vary in color from light to medium green. Some celery ribs have smooth outer surfaces and some are more ridged; the smoother ones tend to have a milder flavor and less tough strings. Never buy celery whose ribs are turning yellow or brown.

Preparation: Rinse ribs well, using a scrub brush. You can discard or use the celery leaves according to taste. I don't juice the leaves, but save them to use in my vegetable broth (page 162).

The juice: 2 large outer celery ribs, trimmed (6 ounces), yield ½ cup of thin juice, with a fairly neutral flavor—neither bitter nor sweet.

Cherries

Cherries come in many varieties, the most commonly available being sweet and dark Bing cherries. Sour cherries, which are a bright red, are available for a short time early in the summer and are usually used for cooking and baking (and unless you really love sour foods, they are not especially well suited to juicing). The Queen Anne cherry, light yellow with a red blush, is very sweet, but has a less intense cherry flavor.

Serving size: 10 medium cherries (2½ ounces)

Nutrition: 52 calories. Cherries are not an outstanding source of any one particular nutrient, although they are a fair source of vitamins C and E (both of which are 8 percent of the RDA) and provide small amounts of most vitamins and minerals.

Season: June, July, and August. Imported cherries can be found in January and February. Frozen unsweetened cherries are available year-round.

Shopping: Look for firm, but not hard cherries that have a nice shiny finish. Green fresh-looking stems indicate fresher cherries than those with dried shriveled stems.

Preparation: Rinse, discard stems, and pit. You must pit every single cherry that you intend to use in your juicer—this job can be made considerably easier if you purchase a cherry pitter (a relatively inexpensive gadget). If using frozen cherries, make sure they're pitted. Measure while frozen; defrost before juicing.

The juice: 11 large cherries, stemmed and pitted (4 ounces), yield ¼ cup of fairly thick juice (a little thicker than nectar), with flavor

55

ranging from sweet to fairly tart depending on the fruit, with a very intense cherry flavor.

Coconut

Coconut is not suitable for juice at all. If you try to juice fresh coconut, you will end up with very finely shredded coconut and a very unhappy juice extractor. For coconut flavor you can stir canned coconut milk or cream into your juice.

Corn

Corn is very high in starch, which makes it chalky and unsuitable for juicing.

Cranberries

Cranberries are so tart a large glass of unsweetened cranberry juice is not much of a treat. However, the tartness does make a nice contrast to the juice of sweet fruits, such as Golden Delicious apple juice.

Serving size: ¼ cup

Nutrition: 12 calories. Cranberries have a fairly good nutritional profile, but because of the tartness we use only a small quantity whose nutritional contribution is negligible.

Season: September to December. Cranberries freeze very well; buy a few bags when they're in season and freeze for use throughout the year.

Shopping: Cranberries are almost always sold packaged in plastic bags. Look for bright color and shiny skin. They should be dry and hard when pressed.

Preparation: Rinse. If frozen, measure them frozen, then defrost partially before juicing.

The juice: ¼ cup of cranberries (1 ounce) yields 1 tablespoon of very, very tart purée.

Cucumbers

Cucumbers are usually waxed (you can tell by the greasy feel); the smaller Kirby (the type used for pickles) is unwaxed; the English (known as burpless), which is very long and usually comes tightly wrapped in plastic, is also unwaxed. Old cucumbers have large, tough, tan seeds (not inedible, just unpleasant).

When preparing cucumbers for the juicer, taste a thin slice from each end to make sure they are both fresh tasting—not bitter. If the end is bitter, keep slicing and tasting until you get to the fresh part; it's rare for a cucumber to be bitter throughout.

57

Serving size: ½ cucumber (5 ounces)

Nutrition: 20 calories for ½ a good-size cucumber. Like celery, cucumber is a favorite with dieters because of its low calorie count. It is a source of selenium (14 percent of RDA), a trace mineral that works with vitamin E as an antioxidant. There is also a fair amount of vitamin C (12 percent of RDA) as well as less significant amounts of most vitamins and minerals.

Season: Year-round

Shopping: Cucumbers should be filled out at both ends. They should feel firm but not hard. Cucumbers that give when pressed are over the hill. They should have a good dark green color (except the Kirby, which is slightly lighter). They should not be too fat or too thin, but somewhere in between. Any with soft spots or wrinkled ends should be avoided.

Preparation: If the cucumbers are waxed they should be peeled; if unwaxed, just rinse and scrub. Taste ends for bitterness.

The juice: 1 medium cucumber, peeled (8 ounces), yields ¾ cup of thin, fairly neutral (though sometimes bitter) juice.

Eggplant

Eggplant is definitely not a vegetable you'll want to juice, since it's very bitter when raw.

Fennel

Fennel, also called sweet or florentine fennel, is a vegetable resembling celery with a licorice flavor. It has a bulbous bottom, which is the part of the vegetable that you juice (or cook). The thick stems and dill-like leaves are often removed before you buy the vegetable.

Serving size: ½ bulb (3 ounces)

Nutrition: Figures are not available.

Season: September to April, although may be found year-round

Shopping: The bulb should not be at all dried out, nor should it be brown. It should be very firm and heavy for its size; if there are leaves on the stalk, they should be moist and fresh looking, not dried out.

Preparation: Discard the stems and leaves and trim a small piece off the bottom of the bulb. Cut into chunks to fit into the chute.

The juice: 1 bulb (6 ounces) yields a generous ⅓ cup of thin, milky juice with a strong licorice flavor.

Grapefruits

Grapefruits, available in both white and pink varieties, can be juiced in your extractor, but they require more preparation than if you simply cut them in half and use a citrus juicer: usually a glass dish with a dome or cone in the center for reaming, or a hand-held reamer available in wood, plastic, or aluminum. Electric citrus juicers are different machines from extractors (although at least one extractor has a citrus attachment).

Serving size: ½ grapefruit

Nutrition: 39 calories. Like all citrus fruits, grapefruits are high in vitamin C (71 percent of RDA), and pink grapefruits tend to have good amounts of vitamin A.

Season: Year-round, although better in the winter

Shopping: Grapefruits should feel heavy and give when squeezed gently. Grapefruits that feel hard usually have thick skin and pith; those tend to be drier and more sour than their thin-skinned cousins. I find that grapefruits that have dark scratchy marks on the skin tend to be sweeter than unblemished fruits, but don't take a grapefruit that has large bruises. I actually bend my own fruit rule about shiny skins and seek slightly dull-skinned grapefruits.

Preparation: Discard skin and seeds before juicing.

The juice: 1 small grapefruit, peeled and seeded (7 ounces), yields a generous ⅓ cup of thin juice that is tart with a characteristic grapefruit bitterness.

Grapes

Grapes can be green, red, or black, and anywhere in between. Some are seedless, others have a fair number of seeds. But size and color aside, grapes are usually a sweet fruit.

Serving size: 12 grapes (1¾ ounces)

Nutrition: 35 calories. A modest amount of vitamin C (9 percent of RDA), and some, but not too much, of the other nutrients.

Season: Different varieties are available throughout the year.

Shopping: Grapes should be firm with a slight give. A bunch with many grapes falling off the stem is old. Grapes will soften and turn dark where they attach to the stem as they begin to rot. The best way to tell if a grape is sweet is to taste one—I know shopkeepers aren't keen on this, but it is the only method I know to test for sweetness.

Preparation: Rinse and remove grapes from the stem. I prefer to use seedless grapes, so the question of what to do with the seeds is a moot point. If you want to juice grapes with seeds you can leave them in the grapes or remove them. Seeding grapes is highly labor intensive and you'll save a lot of time if you buy seedless grapes.

The juice: 2 ounces of grapes (12 to 15 medium) yields 2½ to 3 tablespoons of thin juice that tastes sweet but has a bitter aftertaste from the skin. If you have the patience to skin the grapes, the juice would be very sweet.

Green Beans

Green beans are also called snap or string beans, because you snap the end and/or remove the string before cooking (or juicing). They are a tender variety of kidney beans. Although at one time these were strictly seasonal, now you can find them fresh year-round. The juice has a fairly strong flavor, and not necessarily one that you would want to drink lots of. However, if you have a few leftover beans, you can certainly throw them in with other vegetables you are juicing.

Serving size: 12 medium beans (2 ounces)

Nutrition: 18 calories. A fairly good source of vitamin C at 15 percent of the RDA, with moderate amounts of other nutrients.

Season: Available year-round, but best in the summer

Shopping: Large, pale, or bumpy beans tend to be tough. Look for beans with smooth skin and good green color. They should not be very thick and they should snap when bent. If they are limp or wrinkled, pass them up.

Preparation: Rinse and snap off brown end; you can leave the pointy end on.

The juice: 12 medium beans (2 ounces) yields 1 ounce of thin, fairly bitter juice.

Green Leaves

Green leaves include both lettuces and greens. (Greens are large leaves, tougher than their delicate cousin lettuce.) They share a characteristic bitterness (except iceberg lettuce, which is mild and almost sweet in flavor), ranging from only slightly bitter (beet greens or romaine lettuce) to extremely bitter (dandelion or collard greens). As a rule of thumb, the darker the leaves the more bitter the flavor and the higher the nutrient count.

Season: Year-round

Nutrition: Very good sources of vitamins A and C as well as E, and many important minerals such as iron and calcium.

Shopping: Greens are sold either attached to the root (as in beets) or in bunches without the roots, and lettuces are sold in heads. Look for fresh bright leaves. Avoid greens that are dull looking, wilted, or limp, brown around the edges, or at all slimy.

Preparation: Rinse thoroughly, then fold in half widthwise and fold into a tight package that will fit into the chute of your extractor. If desired, you can juice the stalks too. Just rinse and feed into extractor.

The juice: About 1 tablespoon of juice per ounce of leaves. Tasting the green before you juice it will give you a good idea of how bitter the juice will be. The bitterness of greens seems slightly more prominent in the juice. For example, you don't think of romaine lettuce as being particularly bitter, but that is the dominant flavor of the juice.

Honeydew Melon

Honeydew melon, like all melons, must be ripe for fine taste. But, as with all melons, ripeness is hard to determine.

Serving size: 1 wedge (4 to 5 ounces)

Nutrition: 45 calories. A very good source of vitamin C (53 percent of RDA) and a fairly good source of folacin (10 percent), potassium (9 percent), and thiamin (B_1: 9 percent).

Season: Peak months are July and August, but available year-round.

Shopping: As with cantaloupes, honeydews should be heavy, give a little when pressed at the blossom end, and have seeds that shake. The skin of the melon should not be too white or green but rather creamy in color. If possible, buy a honeydew that has been halved so you can look at the flesh and smell the aroma.

Preparation: Discard rind and seeds before juicing.

The juice: ⅙ of a small honeydew, rind and seeds removed (6 ounces), yields ½ cup of very sweet, thin juice. The flavor is subtle and easily gets lost when combined with fruits or vegetables with a distinct flavor.

Jicama

Jicama, popular in Latin markets, is not a great vegetable to juice because of its high starch content, which gives an unpleasant chalkiness to the drink.

Kiwi

Kiwi, the small oval fruit with the hairy brown exterior and the lush green interior with the beautiful tiny black seeds, is a taste delight.

Serving size: 1 kiwi (2½ to 3 ounces)

Nutrition: 46 calories, providing 124 percent of the RDA for vitamin C, with some but not a lot of other nutrients.

Season: Year-round

Shopping: Like all fruits, kiwis are best when fully ripe. When squeezed gently the fruit should give just a little. Rock-hard kiwis are sour and pale green. If the kiwi gives too much, the fruit is overripe and mushy.

Preparation: Peel before juicing.

The juice: 1 medium kiwi, peeled (2½ ounces), yields 1 ounce (2 tablespoons) of very thick purée, which does not come through the extractor, but must be followed by a thinner juice. It adds thickness and tartness to other juices.

Kohlrabi

Kohlrabi is a member of the cabbage family. It's similar to a beet in size, but has a light green color. Like beets, kohlrabi may be found with or without leaves, and you can juice the leaves if you like. Unlike beets, kohlrabi is not a root, but rather a bulbous part of the stem, therefore it is not grown underground and doesn't have the earthy flavor so frequently associated with root vegetables.

Serving size: 1 medium kohlrabi (4 ounces)

Nutrition: 23 calories. Provides 88 percent of the RDA for vitamin C with some but not much of other nutrients.

Season: Year-round

Shopping: The green skin should have a sheen and the vegetable itself should be quite firm. If the leaves are on the kohlrabi, they should be fresh looking.

Preparation: Trim top; it's not necessary to peel.

The juice: 1 medium kohlrabi, trimmed (4 ounces), yields ¼ cup of thin juice with a mild flavor but bitter aftertaste.

Lemons and Limes

Lemons and limes are wonderful all-around fruits used for flavoring. Too tart to use alone, these juices freshen and/or decrease the sweetness of other fruits and vegetables. Although you can juice them in an extractor, it's probably easier to halve the fruit and squeeze as much juice as you want into your beverage.

Serving size: Since you rarely eat an entire lemon or lime, serving size does not apply.

Nutrition: Like all citrus fruits, lemons and limes are high in vitamin C. However, since you rarely use more than 1 tablespoonful, the amount you get is minimal (about 12 percent of the RDA).

Season: Year-round

Shopping: Shiny skin is very important to tell the freshness of lemons or limes. They should also give a little when pressed. Hard lemons or limes and bumpy skin indicate a thick layer of pith and an underripe fruit, which also indicates little juice.

Preparation: If you choose to use lemons or limes in the extractor, remove the skin and discard seeds before juicing.

The juice: ½ lemon or lime yields about 1 tablespoon of thin, very tart juice (very underripe lemons or limes can yield half as much juice, while very juicy ones can yield twice as much.)

Mangoes

Mangoes have a fragrance like a siren call. This tropical fruit is sweet and juicy, with flesh similar to a perfectly ripe nectarine. In fact, if you can't find mangoes, substitute nectarines.

Serving size: ½ mango (3½ to 4 ounces)

Nutrition: For their 68 calories, mangoes are antioxidant heaven, providing 50 percent of the RDA of vitamin A, 48 percent of vitamin C, and 15 percent of vitamin E.

Season: April to September; imports available in winter

Shopping: Mangoes can range in color from green to yellow; most will have some red blush. A hard mango is definitely unripe. Mangoes should give when gently squeezed, if ripe. Additionally they should have a heavenly aroma. My own preference is for mangoes that are mostly yellow with just some green and/or red on them.

Preparation: Peel mangoes for juicing (using a vegetable parer). I'm sure the machines can cope with the skin, but I'm uncertain about the pesticides used in the countries where they are grown. Removing mango flesh from the seed, especially ripe and juicy flesh, is a fairly messy job. After peeling the mango, cut away the flesh from the pit in large chunks. As you get closer to the pit, the flesh will start to cling and you will encounter a stringy texture. I tend to leave a fair amount of flesh on the seed, and then I just pick up the seed and eat whatever fruit didn't want to be cut away.

The juice: Mango juice is in reality a purée—like baby food. It doesn't come out of the juicer and must be juiced with a fruit or vegetable that produces a thin juice to wash the purée through the extractor.

Mushrooms

Mushrooms are available in an astounding variety. Usually the "wild" mushrooms (I put wild in quotation marks, because many exotic kinds are now being cultivated) are more flavorful than the cultivated white ones. Mushrooms are also available dried, and the flavor of these is the most intense of all; ideal for making soup, but not juice.

A word of caution about picking your own wild mushrooms—some varieties are poisonous and unless you are an expert on mushrooms, I suggest you stick to the varieties you can find in the market.

Serving size: 6 medium mushrooms (4 ounces)

Nutrition: 28 calories. Mushrooms have an incredibly good nutrition profile: 104 percent of the RDA for thiamin (B_1), 39 percent riboflavin (B_2), 33 percent of niacin (B_3), 36 percent of pantothenic acid; 22 percent of copper; 15 percent of phosphorus; 11 percent of potassium; 8 percent of iron; and lesser amounts of other nutrients.

Season: Year-round

Shopping: Always look for mushrooms that are not wet or slimy to the touch, but not so dry as to seem dehydrated. Cultivated mushrooms should not have brown spots. The membrane that covers the depression where cap and stem meet should be attached.

Preparation: Rinse; trim bottoms.

The juice: Mushrooms are a soft vegetable that juice into a purée rather than a liquid. The flavor is distinctly earthy, being neither sour nor bitter. Mushrooms must be combined with a fruit or vegetable that yields a thin juice to wash the purée through the extractor.

Nectarines

Nectarines, a peach's unfuzzy cousin, is juicy with a smooth satiny flesh, similar to mango. They are sweet-tart and great raw or cooked with other fruits.

Serving size: 1 medium nectarine (4½ to 5 ounces)

Nutrition: 67 calories. A fairly good source of vitamin A (13 percent of the RDA) and vitamin C (12 percent), with a fair amount of niacin (B_3: 9 percent) and potassium (8 percent)

Shopping: Nectarines should have a nice sheen to the skin with a deep yellow color and lots of red blush. They should give when lightly pressed. Nectarines seem to ripen from the bottom up so check the color of the skin at the top—it should be the same deep yellow color as the rest of the fruit. If the blossom end is slightly green the nectarine is not yet ripe. Ripe nectarines will also give off an enticing aroma. If you can't smell it, don't buy it.

Season: June, July, August, September; imports are available in December, January, and February.

Preparation: Rinse, halve, and discard pit.

The juice: 1 medium nectarine yields about ⅓ cup of very thick (thinner than a purée, but thicker than nectar) juice that is somewhat tart.

Onions

Onions, as a family, are all sharp tasting. You'll never want to use more than a little in any juice because the onion flavor is so assertive it will dominate the beverage in which it's used. I use onions sparingly —and only with vegetable juices.

All members of the onion family are available year-round. Because only a small amount of onions are used in juicing, the nutritional value is negligible.

Brown or white onions are the common cooking onions. Usually the smaller onions have a sharper flavor. Such large varieties as Bermuda, Spanish, Vidalia, and Maui range from fairly to quite mild. Onions should be firm with no give when pressed; avoid onions that have green shoots coming out the middle. The outer skin will range from a nice uniform brown to a very thin, almost white tissue paper. New onions have thin skin, and as the season continues they develop thicker skins. All are equally good.

Leeks are mild members of the onion family; usually only the white bottoms are used in cooking. Look for leeks that are not wilted, and have no yellow leaves. Leeks are very sandy and should be cut in half lengthwise and rinsed thoroughly to rid them of any grit lurking between the layers. Leeks are not especially valuable for juicing.

Scallions (green onions), smaller than leeks, also have green leaves and a white bottom, but in the scallion both white and green parts are used. They are less sharp than small cooking onions, and some people even eat scallions by themselves as a snack (I find them too sharp for this). Look for scallions that have fresh-looking green tops. If you plan to use them in juice, be sparing.

Shallots taste like a cross between garlic and onions. Choose those that are hard, with a nice shine to the skin and no green shoots coming out the top. They are very strongly flavored and should be used sparingly for juicing.

Oranges

Oranges can be juiced in your extractor, but they require more preparation than if you simply cut them in half and use a citrus juicer. In many recipes I juice them in the extractor so the thinner orange juice can "wash" thicker fruit purées through the machine.

There are two types of oranges commonly available—navel, or eating oranges, and juice oranges. Navels are usually seedless and juice oranges have lots of seeds. A navel has a navel on the bottom, which a juice orange lacks. Additionally, California navel oranges tend to have perfect deep orange skin (although bumpy, not smooth). Florida navels look like juice oranges with a less orange (sometimes even greenish) color, a smooth skin with black "scratch" marks. Although the California navels are more widely distributed and better looking, Floridas are just as delicious.

I find that juice oranges are indeed best for juicing—they're less expensive than navels and produce more juice.

70

Serving size: ½ large or 1 small orange (4¼ to 5 ounces)

Nutrition: 60 calories. Sunshine and vitamin C are the trademarks of oranges and deservedly so with 1 orange providing 116 percent of the RDA for vitamin C, as well as 10 percent of folacin and thiamin (B_1) and lesser amounts of other nutrients.

Season: California—year-round; Florida—November to June

Shopping: Oranges should be heavy for their size and give when gently squeezed. Hard oranges with very bumpy skin usually indicate that the oranges will have a thick pith and not much juice.

Preparation: If using the orange in an extractor, cut off the skin using a sharp knife, then halve widthwise and discard the seeds.

The juice: 1 medium orange, peeled and seeded (5 ounces), yields a generous ¼ cup of sweet, thin, fresh tasting orange juice.

Papaya

Papaya is a tropical fruit that is sometimes green with a little yellow or vice-versa; the greener and harder the papaya, the less ripe.

The interior is the color of a nectarine, although the Hawaiian variety has a coral-orange interior. The center of the papaya is filled with juicy black seeds, which are edible but not particularly tasty. Papaya flesh is tender, but not as juicy as ripe mango, peach, or nectarine. It has a smooth mouth feel and an almost floral flavor.

Serving size: ½ papaya (5 to 5½ ounces)

Nutrition: 59 calories. Papaya provides 157 percent of the RDA for vitamin C; 38 percent for vitamin A, and 10 percent of potassium, as well as lesser amounts of other vitamins and minerals. In addition to the traditional nutrients, papaya contains the enzyme papain, which is extremely helpful in the digestion of protein.

Season: Year-round

Shopping: Look for papayas that are more yellow than green and that give when gently pressed. Avoid papayas with black spots or bruises. They can be purchased underripe and ripened at home.

Preparation: Although you can probably juice the papaya skin, seeds, and all, I don't like the flavor of the seeds and don't want them in my juice. Naturally, I recommend that you discard the seeds. Similarly, although the extractor is capable of dealing with papaya skin, I peel the fruit with a vegetable parer before juicing.

The juice: Like most soft fruits, papaya doesn't come out of the extractor as juice, but rather the consistency of smooth applesauce. (If you wish, combine with a fruit that produces a thin juice to wash

71

it through.) 1 papaya yields about ¾ cup of sauce, which is fragrant and sweet in flavor.

Parsley

Parsley is really a good source of many nutrients. Toss some in with any vegetable juice. There are two types of parsley available: curly and Italian (flat leaf) and they can be used interchangeably.

Serving size: 1 ounce

Nutrition: For just 10 calories you can get 43 percent of your RDA for vitamin C, 18 percent of vitamin A, 13 percent of folacin, and 10 percent of iron, as well as lesser amounts of other nutrients.

Season: Year-round

Shopping: Look for bright green fresh leaves. Pass up any dull, wilted, or yellowed bunches.

Preparation: Rinse.

The juice: 1 tablespoon of juice for 1 ounce of parsley. It's very dark green with a stong "green" flavor, not especially bitter—but not especially pleasant either.

Parsnip

Parsnip is a root more often used as an ingredient in soup than as a vegetable by itself. Eaten or juiced, the parsnip has a strong flavor with a slightly bitter aftertaste. Use just a little parsnip with other vegetables for a fresh flavor.

Serving size: 1 small root (2 ounces)

Nutrition: 43 calories. A great source of pantothenic acid (49 percent of the RDA), 16 percent of vitamin C, 9 percent of folacin, as well as some of various other nutrients.

Season: Year-round

Shopping: Look for firm roots with a light or medium tan skin. Avoid parsnips with soft spots, and those that are limp or wrinkled.

Preparation: Scrub well and discard top.

The juice: 1 large parsnip (6 ounces) yields a scant ¼ cup of thin juice. It has a mild, fresh flavor, but leaves a bitter aftertaste. It's good mixed with other juices.

Peaches

Peaches are one of summer's great treats. To be referred to as "a real peach" is a compliment to relish. Peaches can be peach color or white, freestone or cling; no matter what the variety, when ripe they are delicious. Frozen unsweetened peaches are available year-round.

Peaches darken when exposed to air, so don't make juices with them until just before serving.

Serving size: 1 small peach (3 ounces)

Nutrition: 37 calories. Peaches are not a great source of any one nutrient, but they have a moderate amount of vitamin E (11 percent of the RDA) and vitamin C (9 percent).

Season: June to September; imported peaches in December, January, or February

Shopping: Look for peaches with peach color and lots of red blush. The fruit should be peach or red at the top around the stem; if that area is green the peach is underripe. Also, the peach should give

73

when gently pressed, and, most important, you should be able to smell that great peach fragrance.

Preparation: Rinse, halve, and discard pit.

The juice: 1 small peach, pitted (3 ounces), yields a scant ¼ cup of very thick juice that is sweet with a slightly tart aftertaste.

Pears

Pears can be red, green, yellow, and brown. Like apples and other low-acid fruits, pears oxidize and turn brown quickly; therefore, juices containing them should be prepared just before serving.

Serving size: ½ pear (3 ounces)

Nutrition: 49 calories. Pears are not especially high in any particular nutrient, but have some small amount of most of them.

Season: Year-round

Shopping: Pears are usually underripe (hard) when sold; they should be ripened at home. Avoid pears (ripe or underripe) that have blemishes or bruises. A ripe pear should give a little when pressed at the top. A soft bottom may indicate a rotten core. A fragrant aroma is also a sign of a ripe pear.

Preparation: Rinse and halve, discard core and stem.

The juice: An underripe pear produces a juice similar in consistency to fruit nectar, whereas a ripe pear produces more of a purée. One underripe pear, cored (6 ounces), yields ⅓ cup juice. For a ripe pear, it is necessary to juice another fruit or vegetable that yields thin juice to wash the pear purée through. Pear flavor is delicate and gets easily lost in mixtures of strongly flavored fruits or vegetables.

Peas

Peas are among those starchy vegetables that are best cooked and not juiced.

Peppers

Peppers come in two types: sweet and hot. Add fresh hot peppers to juice at your own discretion—keeping in mind that the heat is in the seeds, and you may want to remove some or all of them before adding to the juicer.

Sweet peppers—red, orange, yellow, green, and purple—have an assertive flavor and, like onions, dominate the flavor of any juice they're in, so it's best to use just a small amount. The red and orange peppers are the sweetest. Yellow is somewhat sweeter than a green, but basically is similar in flavor, and the green and purple taste pretty much alike. The only difference is that the purples tend to have a tougher skin (purple peppers are green on the inside, like ordinary green peppers). The seeds of the sweet bell pepper are mild and will not affect the juice. I discard them because they make the pulp unusable.

Serving size: ½ small pepper (1½ ounces)

Nutrition: Only 9 calories, yet 79 percent of the RDA for vitamin C, and fair amounts of other nutrients. Red peppers have even higher amounts of C (118 percent), and also provide 26 percent of the RDA for vitamin A.

Season: Green peppers are available year-round; the rest are plentiful in late summer and imported (at much higher prices) during the rest of the year.

75

Shopping: The rule with peppers is: the deeper the color, the stronger the flavor. Look for peppers that are firm; if they give at all they are not as fresh as you'd like. They should not have dark patches, nor should they be wrinkled. Also, choose peppers that feel heavy.

Preparation: Rinse, halve the pepper, and discard pithy center with seeds and stem.

The juice: ½ bell pepper, stem and seeds removed (3½ ounces), yields a generous ⅓ cup of thin juice. The juice from red peppers tends to be sweet, whereas the green peppers are more pungent.

Pineapples

Pineapples have a tough skin, but many supermarkets now have machines that remove the flesh from the skin. This is good news for shoppers who don't want to bother cutting up the fruit, and it also allows you to see and smell the fruit's ripeness.

Serving size: ⅛ medium pineapple (4 ounces)

Season: Year-round

Nutrition: 56 calories. The best profile is for vitamin C (29 percent of the RDA), and 10 percent of thiamin (B_1).

Shopping: Look for pineapples that are primarily golden colored with just a little green. They should give a little when pressed, but not be too soft since that would indicate an overripe pineapple. Another test is to pull a leaf from the top; if it comes out easily, the fruit is ripe. A ripe pineapple should have a mild aroma; if you can't smell anything, it may be underripe; a strong aroma may mean it's overripe.

If you are buying pineapple that has its rind removed, look for a medium yellow color and a fragrant aroma. Very dark yellow indicates overripe and very light yellow is underripe.

Preparation: Discard tops and remove rind.

The juice: ¼ large pineapple, rind removed (12 ounces), yields about ⅞ cup of thin, sweet/tart juice.

Plums

Plums are usually sweet-tart—more sweet when ripe, and more tart when underripe. There are purple plums with red or yellow flesh; red skin with red or yellow flesh; greengages, which are green skinned with yellow flesh, and Italian plums, sometimes called prunes, which are small, purple, and oval.

Serving size: 1 large or 2 small plums (2 to 2½ ounces)

Nutrition: 36 calories. Plums have only a modest amount of vitamins and minerals, with vitamin C topping the list at 11 percent of the RDA.

Season: May to September

Shopping: Plums should be fairly soft when gently pressed, but not too soft—if they feel bloated they are too soft. Hard plums are definitely underripe. Greengages and Italian (fresh prune) plums, which both have very short seasons, lack some of the tartness of other varieties.

Preparation: Rinse, halve, and pit.

The juice: 1 large plum, pitted (4 ounces), yields about ¼ cup of juice the thickness of nectar, with a sweet-tart flavor.

Pomegranates

Pomegranates, available only in the fall, are poor candidates for the juice extractor because the fruit is made up of small seeds that are difficult and messy to separate from the bitter rind. Pomegranate juice can be made by using a home press, like one used for citrus juices. Pomegranates are quite tart in flavor. Grenadine, which is made of a pomegranate juice base, is largely sugar.

Potatoes

Potatoes, like jicama or any other highly starchy vegetable, make an unpleasant beverage, which to my mind defeats the purpose of making juice.

 78

Radishes

Radishes are available in the familiar red variety, small and round, as well as white, which are finger size, and daikon, which are also white but tend to be quite large, and black radishes. All radishes have a sharp peppery bite to them, with red and black being slightly sharper than the whites.

Serving size: 4 medium radishes (¾ ounce)

Nutrition: Not a lot of nutrients in radishes—but for 3 calories you can't ask for the world.

Season: Year-round

Shopping: Look for radishes that are very firm; pass up any that give at all. Red radishes are available in cello bags or with the leaves on. When possible buy the bunches with the leaves, so you can check for freshness.

Preparation: Rinse and discard leaves or remains of stems.

The juice: Hot or spicy only begins to describe the tongue-tingling effect that radish juice has on your throat. Use it sparingly to spice up dull drinks. 2 to 3 medium radishes, tops and roots trimmed (2 ounces), yield 1 ounce of thin, very spicy, lavender (if you're using red radishes) juice.

Raspberries

Raspberries, the most elegant of berries, come in red and black (not to be confused with blackberries, which are larger and longer). Red raspberries are commonly available, while the black ones are rarely on the market.

Serving size: ½ cup (3 ounces)

Nutrition: 42 calories. Raspberries have a good amount of vitamin C (35 percent of RDA), with lesser amounts of other nutrients.

Season: June to September and December to February

Shopping: As with blackberries, you must be careful to avoid moldy berries. Check the bottom of the container as well as the top and give it a good sniff to make sure there's no mold lurking in the basket. Raspberries can be quite tart or quite sweet and I don't know how to determine which basket is which, except to try to stick to the peak of raspberry season, and then cross your fingers.

Preparation: Rinse.

The juice: ½ cup raspberries (3 ounces) yields about 2 tablespoons of very thick saucelike juice.

79

Spinach

Spinach has an excellent nutritional profile, as do most greens. Pop-eye knew what he was doing when he ate his spinach to keep strong. You can find spinach with a relatively flat leaf (medium green), or tufted and very dark green.

Bunches of fresh spinach are frequently small clumps of spinach held together by a rubber band. I measure the spinach in these recipes by clump, which means if you held one root in your hand it would be like a mini lettuce with some large outer leaves and some small inner ones. Each clump weighs about 1½ ounces.

Spinach is sometimes sold in cello bags, but I prefer to buy in bulk. In either case, be sure to rinse spinach thoroughly because it can be quite sandy.

Serving size: 2 to 3 clumps, roots trimmed (4 ounces)

Nutrition: A nutrition bargain. For 25 calories you get 95 percent of the RDA for vitamin A; 55 percent for folacin, 53 percent for pantothenic acid, 38 percent for vitamin E, 30 percent for magnesium, 17 percent for potassium, 17 percent for iron, 16 percent for riboflavin ($B_2$2), 11 percent for pyridoxine (B_6), and lesser amounts of other nutrients.

Season: Year-round

Shopping: Look for bright fresh leaves with no wilt at all.

Preparation: Discard the bottoms of the stems and rinse leaves extremely well.

The juice: 4 ounces of spinach yields ⅓ cup of thin, dark green juice, which is fairly neutral in flavor but has a hint of chalkiness.

Squash

Squash comes in two distinct types: winter and summer. Winter squash is a thick-skinned hard vegetable, with well-developed seeds, not suitable for use raw. All varieties are excellent cooked but are not suitable for juicing.

Summer squash is thin skinned and can be eaten raw as well as cooked. I haven't included any summer squash juice in my recipes because I haven't come up with any recipe that I liked. But this is a matter of taste and you may want to experiment on your own.

Serving size: ½ cup cubed winter squash or 1 cup sliced summer squash

Nutrition: ½ cup cubed winter squash contains 40 calories; 1 cup sliced summer squash has 26 calories. Winter squash is a fair source of vitamin A and is treated as a complex carbohydrate. Summer squash is not a great source of any particular vitamin or mineral.

Shopping: Summer squashes should have shiny skin (dull means old) and be firm and heavy for their size; oversize squashes are less tasty.

Strawberries

Strawberries are now available year-round, but the difference between locally grown summer berries and those available throughout most of the year is the degree of sweetness and the texture. Wild strawberries, occasionally available in the summer, tend to be significantly smaller than cultivated berries and have a much more intense flavor.

When using strawberries for juicing, it's safe to pair them with sweeter fruits and count the strawberry as a tart one.

Serving size: 1 cup (5 ounces)

Nutrition: 45 calories. Strawberries provide your total RDA of vitamin C (107 percent), but only modest amounts of the remaining nutrients.

Season: Year-round

Shopping: The deeper the color, the sweeter the strawberry (however, too dark and the berries are overripe). Avoid strawberries that are white at the top, around or under the leaves, as these are underripe. For freshness, check the leaves and the skin of the berry. The leaves should be green and not dried out. The skin should have a shiny appearance—a dull finish indicates berries too long off the plant (they may still be flavorful and they are not rotten). They should also feel firm, but not hard. Rotten berries will be moldy and have bruises or soft dark areas.

Preparation: Rinse and hull berries.

The juice: 6 large strawberries or 10 medium (6 ounces) yield about ⅔ cup of very thick, tart juice.

Tomatoes

Tomatoes are one of the most important elements in many cuisines (alongside onions, garlic, potatoes, and olive oil). Botanically, tomatoes are fruits rather than vegetables. They come in many sizes and shapes, even two colors, red and yellow. Yellow tomatoes were developed for a low acid content.

All tomatoes are suitable for eating raw or for cooking, although some tend to be used more for one than the other. For instance, cherry tomatoes (which are round and the size of cherries) are usually tossed into salads, raw. Plum (Italian) and pear tomatoes, which are elongated, tend to be used for cooking. The larger round tomatoes are used either way.

Serving size: 1 small tomato (4 to 4½ ounces)

Nutrition: 24 calories. A good source of vitamin C (36 percent of the RDA) and fairly good of vitamin A (17 percent) and E (11 percent), with lesser amounts of the remaining nutrients.

Season: Year-round

Shopping: Fortunately, tomatoes ripen extremely well at home; just leave underripe tomatoes at room temperature until ripe. The ideal tomato has a deep red color. The more you allow tomatoes to ripen, the more the flavor develops (but like the strawberry, too dark and the tomato is about to become overripe). Ripe tomatoes should not have brown or black areas, which would indicate that they're over the hill. Underripe tomatoes tend to be more orange in color and firm when gently pressed. Ripe tomatoes will give a little when pressed.

Preparation: Rinse; if the tomato has a stem and leaves, discard them.

The juice: 1 medium tomato (6 ounces) yields a generous ½ cup of moderately thick juice with a very fresh tomato flavor—very different from canned tomato juice.

Turnips

Turnips, when cooked, are not noticeably bitter, but raw turnip juice is quite undrinkable.

Watermelons

Watermelons are now available in varieties different from the huge ones of yesteryear. You can buy them the size of a honeydew with red or yellow flesh, with or without seeds. But I find the large ones sweeter.

When buying a cut watermelon, look for one that has a deep pink color (if the color is a brownish pink it's too ripe or bruised). Pale pink watermelons tend to have less flavor than the darker ones. Look for melons that don't have a lot of white "strings" or "cracks" in the flesh itself. The flesh should be even in color and surface texture. Uncut watermelon should be heavy for their size and have no bruises or cuts; then hope for the best.

Serving size: ¾-inch-thick wedge (6 ounces).

Nutrition: 50 calories. A good source of vitamin C (26 percent of the RDA), and fairly good source of thiamin (B_1: 12 percent) and pyridoxine (B_6: 11 percent), as well as lesser amounts of the other nutrients.

Season: Year-round

Preparation: You can juice watermelon, rind and all, but my preference is to discard the rind and juice just the red flesh. This is one fruit where I leave the seeds in.

The juice: A ¾-inch wedge, rind removed (6 ounces), yields about ½ cup of fairly thin, sweet juice.

Food Combining for Juicing

There are three factors involved in choosing foods to combine in juices: theoretical, nutritional, and practical.

Starting with the theoretical: There are some people who suggest that for health reasons, fruits and vegetables should not be juiced together; and/or certain vegetable juices should not be taken in large doses.

The logic behind food-combining theories is that the body works most efficiently when it has to cope with only one type of food at a time because different types of foods (carbohydrates, proteins, fats, acid or sugary foods) are digested at different rates. However, digestion is largely accomplished by enzymes, each one specific to a particular food: Lactase (an enzyme) breaks down only lactose (milk sugar), no matter what other foods are present. This is true of all enzymes, and they do not get confused by the presence of other foods.

But if you still feel that combining fruits and vegetables is not a good idea, there is no reason that you have to combine them. Just follow the recipes for one or the other category and skip the ones that are combination drinks (the recipes are conveniently divided into those categories).

As for not drinking more than one or two ounces of "powerful" drinks—specifically dark green beverages or beet juice, again, I know of no scientific studies that support these claims. Most dark green juices do have strong flavors that benefit greatly by being diluted with more neutral flavored juices, so in the end I come up with the same advice but for different reasons. If after drinking certain fruit or vegetable juices, you begin to feel ill, your heart races, or you have other adverse effects, my guess is that you may be having an allergic reaction and should avoid the offending beverage, fruit or vegetable, in the future. Or you might consult an allergist.

Nutritionally, my thought on combining juices is that, as in all things, variety is the key. If you drink the same juice day after day, you will be getting only a limited number of vitamins and minerals. By juicing a combination of fruits and/or vegetables, you benefit from a well-rounded nutrient profile. I find that combining fruits and vegetables offers the advantage that fruits can be used to improve palatability of vegetable drinks; and vegetables increase the volume of fruit drinks without adding too many extra calories.

In addition to drinking a variety of juices, be sensible about how much you drink of any one type of juice. If you wouldn't eat two pounds of carrots at one sitting, don't drink the equivalent of two pounds of carrots in one sitting either. I like to limit my intake to no more than two servings of any individual fruit or vegetable in one drink.

One word of caution about drinking straight fruit juices: They are high in sugar (even though it's a natural form of sugar) and it gets metabolized very quickly, giving you a quick "sugar high," followed by a "low." If you are diabetic, or suspect that you have problems with sugar metabolism, consult your doctor before starting a juice regimen that includes large amounts of fruit juices.

The practical factors include flavor, texture, and availability. I stongly believe that drinking juice should be a pleasant experience. Fruits and vegetables that taste terrible don't belong in your glass, unless you've found a way to combine them with something that makes the juice palatable (or better yet, delicious).

As for the second factor, texture and consistency, some fruits and vegetables become more of a purée than a juice. When using these you will have to pair them with fruits or vegetables that make thin juice, to make the purée a drinkable consistency. First juice the fruit or vegetable that produces the thick purée, follow it with the vegetable or fruit that produces thin juices, thereby "washing" the thick juice through the machine.

Availability can mean "in season" or "in the refrigerator." Although nowadays many fruits and vegetables are "in season" year-round, the true season (e.g., watermelon in summer rather than November) is when you'll find produce at its flavor peak (and have the added bonus of lower prices).

More likely it's "what's in the refrigerator" that will guide your choice. Some staples that I always keep on hand are apples, beets, carrots, celery, and cucumbers. These vegetables and fruits tend to combine well with most flavors and also produce thin juice that is a desirable juicing trait.

The following chart will help you pick compatible combinations. Try to pair tart items with sweet, bitter with neutral or sweet, and thick with thin. Of course, sweet and neutral items also combine well with each other and two thin juices can make a delicious combination.

	SWEET	TART *	BITTER	SPICY	NEUTRAL **
THIN	Apple Beet Blueberry Cantaloupe Carrot Honeydew Pineapple Watermelon	Apple Blueberry Grape Lemon Lime	Asparagus Bean Sprout Grapefruit Green Bean Greens Kohlrabi Turnip	Cabbage Hot Pepper Radish	Bell Pepper Celery Cauliflower Cucumber Fennel Parsley Spinach
MEDIUM	Cherry	Nectarine Plum			Broccoli Tomato
THICK	Banana Mango Papaya Peach Pear Strawberry	Apricot Blackberry Cranberry Kiwi Raspberry Strawberry			Avocado Mushroom

* Some fruits listed as "tart" may also be "sweet" when properly ripened (such as strawberries), but are usually sold underripe or out of season and are therefore placed in the tart column.
** Neutral does not mean flavorless, but rather that the flavor is neither bitter nor spicy (peppery).

Since one of the important assets of fresh juice is its valuable nutritional contribution, it makes sense to use fruits and vegetables with high nutritional profiles. The table below highlights those fruits and vegetables that contain exceptional amounts of the stated vitamins or minerals.

	SUPERSTARS (80–100 + % RDA)	HEROES (50–80% RDA)	HONORABLE MENTION (25–50% RDA)
VITAMIN A	Broccoli Carrot Dandelion greens Spinach	Beet greens Cantaloupe Kale Mango Papaya	Bok choy Mustard greens Red bell pepper
VITAMIN C	Cantaloupe Cauliflower Kale Kohlrabi Orange Papaya Bell peppers Strawberries	Dandelion greens Bok choy Grapefruit Honeydew Mango Mustard greens Spinach	Asparagus Blackberries Pineapple Tomato Watermelon

	SUPERSTARS (80–100 + % RDA)	HEROES (50–80% RDA)	HONORABLE MENTION (25–50% RDA)
VITAMIN B₁	Mushrooms		
VITAMIN B₂			Mushrooms
VITAMIN B₆			Banana
VITAMIN E		Kale	Spinach
FOLACIN		Spinach	Beet
PANTOTHENIC ACID		Parsnip	Mushrooms
MAGNESIUM			Spinach

PART II

Recipes

Using the Recipes

It's good to keep in mind that fresh juice is best when consumed as soon as it's prepared. Although you can store juices in the refrigerator for a day or two, they lose some of the flavor and the foam that is typical of juice fresh from the extractor. Stored juice will frequently separate, leaving a watery substance on the bottom and a denser layer on top. Just stir or shake the juice to restore it to its homogenized state. Further, some fruits that oxidize easily (bananas, apples, pears) will turn the juice brown if left standing for more than a few minutes. This discoloration doesn't affect flavor, but it does make the drink less appealing.

Juices taste best when slightly chilled. I achieve this by refrigerating the fruits and vegetables before juicing. You can serve fresh juice over ice, but it really diminishes the flavor.

Sometimes you may find yourself juicing less than perfectly ripe fruit. The resulting juice could be too tart for your taste and may require some sweetening. Any sweetener you like is acceptable: sugar, honey, fructose, maple syrup, or artificial sweeteners. If you are using sugar, superfine or bar sugar is slightly better than granulated because it dissolves more quickly. Confectioners' sugar is not acceptable because it contains cornstarch, which will add a slight chalkiness to the flavor of the drink.

Because juicing is not an exact art, the weights and sizes of the fruits and vegetables you use will not have to be exactly the same as I've stated in the recipe. I've given both size and weight as guidelines, but the important factor is that the recipes are for compatible combinations of fruits and vegetables. If you prefer to follow the recipes using the weights, your results will be the same as mine. If you are eyeballing a medium or large piece of fruit, your guess of size may be slightly different from mine, and therefore your yield may vary from that given.

In describing weights and sizes, remember that nature is not exact and does not create all produce in separate and distinct categories that can be clearly named large, medium, and small. There are carrots smaller than 2 ounces I've allotted for "small" and carrots larger than the 6 ounces I've designated as "large," and, of course, there are all the weights in between. For example, should a 5-ounce carrot be considered medium (4 ounces) or large? The answer is, for juicing, it doesn't matter too much. Just try to keep the proportions similar to those I've indicated. If a recipe calls for 8 ounces of apple and 4 of pineapple, your juice should be composed of approximately twice as much apple as pineapple.

Finally, there's the question of whether to juice oranges in an extractor or to use a reamer. A reamer is certainly easier to use, since all the preparation needed is to cut the orange in half. An extractor, on the other hand, requires removing the rind completely before cutting the orange into pieces the size of the chute. Another advantage is that the reamer produces a slightly larger volume of juice than the extractor. If you are just making orange juice, the reamer is the right machine to use. If you are using orange juice with a combination of other fruits or vegetables prepared in the extractor, I prefer to juice the orange in the extractor, thereby having to clean only one machine. Further, when the oranges are coupled with soft fruits that require "washing" through the extractor, the juice from the orange is important for this function. If you are combining the orange juice with thin juices, you can opt to use a reamer for the oranges and the extractor for the other fruits or vegetables (see page 89 for a chart of thick and thin juices).

Fruit Juices

Very Strawberry

- 6 large strawberries (hulled: 6 ounces)
- 1 medium juice orange (peeled and seeded: 5 ounces)

Juice in the order of the listed ingredients.

Makes about ¾ cup

The PineApple

- 1 large Golden Delicious apple (cored: 8 ounces)
- ¼ pineapple (rind removed: 7 ounces)

Juice in the order of the listed ingredients.

Makes about 1 cup

Raspberry Sherbet

- ½ cup raspberries (3 ounces)
- ⅙ honeydew (seeds and rind removed: 8 ounces)

Juice in the order of the listed ingredients.

Makes about ⅔ cup

Papaya Julius

- ¼ papaya (peeled and seeded: 3½ ounces)
- ¼ pineapple (rind removed: 7 ounces)

Juice in the order of the listed ingredients.

Makes about ¾ cup

Orangeberry Blue

- ¾ cup blueberries (4 ounces)
- 1 medium juice orange (peeled and seeded: 5 ounces)

Juice in the order of the listed ingredients.

Makes about ½ cup

Evening Sunset

- 7 medium strawberries (hulled: 4 ounces)
- ¼ small cantaloupe (seeds and rind removed: 4 ounces)

Juice in the order of the listed ingredients.

Makes about ⅔ cup

Banana-Orange Juice

- ½ medium banana (peeled: 2 ounces)
- 2 medium juice oranges (peeled and seeded: 5 ounces each)

Juice in the order of the listed ingredients.

Makes about ⅔ cup

 ### Creamsicle

- 2 medium juice oranges (peeled and seeded: 5 ounces each)
- ⅛ pineapple (rind removed: 3½ ounces)

Juice in the order of the listed ingredients.

Makes about 1 cup

Plum Good Apple Juice

- 2 medium plums (pitted: 6 ounces)
- 1 large Golden Delicious apple (cored: 8 ounces)

Juice in the order of the listed ingredients.

Makes about 1 cup

Strawberry Fuzz

- 1 medium peach (pitted: 6 ounces)
- 6 large strawberries (hulled: 6 ounces)

Juice in the order of the listed ingredients.

Makes about 1 cup

Orange Snap

- 2 medium juice oranges, peeled and seeded (5 ounces each)
- 1 slice fresh ginger (the size of a quarter)

Juice 1 orange, then add ginger to extractor. Juice remaining orange.

Makes about ⅔ cup

Minty Hawaiian

- ¼ pineapple (rind removed: 7 ounces)
- 4 sprigs fresh mint, or to taste

Juice half of the pineapple, then the mint, followed by the remaining pineapple.

Makes about ¾ cup

Pineapple-Pear Buzz

- 1 medium pear (cored: 6 ounces)
- ⅛ pineapple (rind removed: 3½ ounces)

Juice in order of the listed ingredients.

Makes about ⅔ cup

Papaya-Apple Drink

- ¼ papaya (peeled and seeded: 3½ ounces)
- 1 medium McIntosh apple (cored: 6 ounces)

Juice in order of the listed ingredients.

Makes about ⅔ cup

Summer Madness

- 1 medium nectarine (pitted: 4 ounces)
- ¼ small cantaloupe (seeds and rind removed: 4 ounces)

Juice in the order of the listed ingredients.

Makes about ⅔ cup

Apple-Bog

- 1 large Golden Delicious apple (cored: 8 ounces)
- ¼ cup cranberries (1 ounce)

Juice half the apple, then the cranberries, followed by the remaining apple.

Makes about ½ cup

WaterBerry

- ¾-inch wedge watermelon (rind removed: 6 ounces)
- ¼ medium cantaloupe (seeds and rind removed: 6 ounces)
- 6 large strawberries (hulled: 6 ounces)

Juice in the order of the listed ingredients.

Makes about 1 cup

Foamy Refresher

- ½ medium banana (peeled: 2 ounces)
- 1 medium kiwi (peeled: 2½ ounces)
- 1 large Golden Delicious apple, cored (8 ounces)

Juice in the order of the listed ingredients.

Makes about ¾ cup

Nectarine Sweetheart

- ¼ cup raspberries (1½ ounces)
- 1 medium nectarine (pitted: 4 ounces)
- 1 medium juice orange (peeled and seeded: 5 ounces)

Juice in the order of the listed ingredients.

Makes about ½ cup

Apple Tart

- ⅓ cup blackberries (2 ounces)
- 1 small apricot (pitted: 1 ounce)
- 1 medium Golden Delicious apple (cored: 6 ounces)

Juice in the order of the listed ingredients.

Makes about 1 cup

Tropical Nectar

- ¼ papaya (peeled and seeded: 3½ ounces)
- Passion fruit seeds (shell discarded)
- ¼ pineapple (rind removed: 7 ounces)

Juice in the order of the listed ingredients.

Makes about ¾ cup

Pomme du Berry

109

- 1 cup blueberries (6 ounces)
- ½ cup raspberries (3 ounces)
- ½ medium Golden Delicious apple (cored: 3 ounces)

Juice in the order of the listed ingredients.

Makes about 1 cup

Banana-Mango-Strawberry Nectar

- ½ medium banana (peeled: 2 ounces)
- ½ mango (peeled and seeded: 3 ounces)
- 6 large strawberries (hulled: 6 ounces)

Juice in the order of the listed ingredients.

Makes about ¾ cup

Berry Berry Apple

110

- ½ cup raspberries (3 ounces)
- 1 cup blueberries (6 ounces)
- ½ medium Golden Delicious apple (cored: 3 ounces)

Juice in the order of the listed ingredients.

Makes about ¾ cup

I Think I Died and Went to Heaven

- ½ medium banana (peeled: 2 ounces)
- ½ papaya (peeled and seeded: 7 ounces)
- 1 medium juice orange (peeled and seeded: 5 ounces)

Juice in the order of the listed ingredients.

Makes about ¾ cup

Grapple

- ½ medium pear (cored: 3 ounces)
- 15 small black grapes (stems removed: 2 ounces)
- 1 medium Golden Delicious apple (cored: 6 ounces)

Juice in the order of the listed ingredients.

Makes about 1 cup

Summer Waker-Upper

- 1 medium grapefruit (peeled and seeded: 7 ounces)
- ⅙ honeydew (seeds and rind removed: 8 ounces)
- ¼ large apple (cored: 2 ounces)

Juice in the order of the listed ingredients.

Makes about ⅔ cup

Sweet-Tart Berry Nectar

- ⅓ cup blackberries (2 ounces)
- ⅓ cup blueberries (2 ounces)
- 15 medium green seedless grapes (stems removed: 4 ounces)

Juice in the order of the listed ingredients.

Makes about ⅔ cup

Banana-Apricot-Orange Squeeze

- ½ medium banana (peeled: 2 ounces)
- 1 large apricot (pitted: 2 ounces)
- 1 medium juice orange (peeled and seeded: 5 ounces)

Juice in the order of the listed ingredients.

Makes about ¾ cup

Tropical Dawn

113

- 1 large kiwi (peeled: 3 ounces)
- 6 large strawberries (hulled: 6 ounces)
- ½ orange (peeled and seeded: 2½ ounces)
- ¼ pineapple (rind removed: 7 ounces)

Juice in the order of the listed ingredients.

Makes about 1 cup

Vegetable Juices

Popeye Power

- 3 large clumps spinach (bottoms trimmed: 4 ounces)
- 1 medium tomato (6 ounces)

Juice in the order of the listed ingredients.

Makes about ¾ cup

Carrot-Celery Booster

- 1 large carrot (top trimmed: 6 ounces)
- 2 medium celery ribs (trimmed: 4 ounces)

Juice in the order of the listed ingredients.

Makes about ⅔ cup

Cucumber Green

- 1 medium cucumber (peeled if waxed: 7 ounces)
- 2 ounces greens (beet, collard, kale, spinach, or similar)

Juice in the order of the listed ingredients.

Makes about ⅔ cup

116 ### Red Rebounder

- ½ medium red pepper (stem, pith, and seeds removed: 3½ ounces)
- 1 medium tomato (6 ounces)

Juice in the order of the listed ingredients.

Makes about ¾ cup

Celery-Tomato Juice

- 1 medium tomato (6 ounces)
- 2 medium celery ribs (trimmed: 4 ounces)

Juice in the order of the listed ingredients.

Makes about 1 cup

Carrot-Cauliflower Plunge

- ¼ small head cauliflower (leaves discarded: 4 ounces)
- 1 large carrot (trimmed: 6 ounces)

Juice in the order of the listed ingredients.

Makes about ⅔ cup

Tomato Slaw

- 1 small cabbage wedge (3 ounces)
- 1 medium tomato (6 ounces)

Juice in the order of the listed ingredients.

Makes about ⅔ cup

Broccoli Booster

- 1 small broccoli stalk (bottom trimmed: 4 ounces)
- 1 medium tomato (6 ounces)

Juice in the order of the listed ingredients.

Makes about ¾ cup

Celery-Beet Juice

- 1 medium beet (trimmed: 4 ounces)
- 2 large outer celery ribs (trimmed: 6 ounces)

Juice in the order of the listed ingredients.

Makes about ⅔ cup

Carroty Cabbage

- 1 small cabbage wedge (3 ounces)
- 1 large carrot (top trimmed: 6 ounces)

Juice in the order of the listed ingredients.

Makes about ½ cup

Broccoli-Celery Smash

- 1 small broccoli stalk (bottom trimmed: 4 ounces)
- 2 medium celery ribs (trimmed: 4 ounces)

Juice in the order of the listed ingredients.

Makes about ½ cup

Tomato Italiano

- 1 large tomato (10 ounces)
- 6 sprigs fresh basil (¼ ounce)
- 8 sprigs fresh parsley (½ ounce)

Juice half the tomato. Add the basil and parsley; juice remaining tomato.

Makes about ¾ cup

C-B-C Juicer Upper

- 1 small broccoli stalk (4 ounces)
- 1 large carrot, trimmed (6 ounces)
- ½ medium cucumber (peeled if waxed: 3½ ounces)

Juice in the order of the listed ingredients.

Makes about ⅔ cup

Lettuce and Tomato Juice

121

- 2 large outer leaves romaine lettuce (2 ounces)
- 1 small wedge iceberg lettuce (2 ounces)
- 1 medium tomato (6 ounces)

Juice in the order of the listed ingredients.

Makes about ⅔ cup

VegeJuice

- 6 medium mushrooms (bottoms trimmed: 4 ounces)
- 1 medium tomato (6 ounces)
- 1 large outer celery rib (trimmed: 3 ounces)

Juice in the order of the listed ingredients.

Makes about ¾ cup

Carrot-Parsley-Parsnip Cocktail

- 1 medium parsnip (top trimmed: 3 ounces)
- 8 sprigs parsley (including stems: ½ ounce)
- 2 medium carrots (tops trimmed: 8 ounces)

Juice in the order of the listed ingredients.

Makes about ½ cup

Tomato Celery Zinger

- 1 large outer celery rib (trimmed: 3 ounces)
- 1 fresh jalapeño pepper (seeded)
- 1 medium tomato (8 ounces)

Juice in the order of the listed ingredients.

Makes about ¾ cup

VegeBreak

123

- 1 medium beet (trimmed: 4 ounces)
- 1 medium celery rib (trimmed: 2 ounces)
- ½ medium cucumber (peeled if waxed: 3½ ounces)

Juice in the order of the listed ingredients.

Makes about ¾ cup

Muddy Waters

- 2 to 3 clumps spinach (bottoms trimmed: 3 ounces)
- 1 medium tomato (6 ounces)
- 1 large outer celery rib (trimmed: 3 ounces)

Juice in the order of the listed ingredients.

Makes about 1 cup

Whole Beet and Carrot Juice

124

- 3 large beet leaves (including stems: 2 ounces)
- 1 medium beet (trimmed: 4 ounces)
- 1 large carrot (top trimmed: 6 ounces)

Juice in the order of the listed ingredients.

Makes about ¾ cup

Herbed Cucumber Juice

- 1 medium cucumber (peeled if waxed: 7 ounces)
- 10 sprigs dill (roots removed: ½ ounce)
- 8 sprigs parsley (including stems: ½ ounce)

Juice half the cucumber, add dill and parsley to the extractor, then juice remaining cucumber.

Makes about ¾ cup

Salad Delight

- 2 large outer leaves romaine lettuce (2 ounces)
- 1 medium carrot (trimmed: 4 ounces)
- ½ medium cucumber (peeled if waxed: 3½ ounces)

Juice in the order of the listed ingredients.

Makes about ¾ cup

Morning Glory

- 1 small beet (trimmed: 2 ounces)
- 3 to 4 clumps spinach (bottoms trimmed: 4 ounces)
- 1 large carrot (top trimmed: 6 ounces)
- 1 medium celery rib (trimmed: 2 ounces)

Juice in the order of the listed ingredients.

Makes about 1 cup

Not So Bloody Mary

- ¼ small lemon (peeled and seeded: 1 ounce)
- 1 large tomato (10 ounces)
- 1½ teaspoons prepared horseradish
- Dash of Worcestershire sauce
- Celery salt, if desired

Juice the lemon, then the tomato. Transfer to a glass and stir in horseradish, Worcestershire sauce, and celery salt.

Makes about ¾ cup

Firecracker

- ¼ medium cauliflower (5 ounces)
- ½ medium cucumber (peeled if waxed: 3½ ounces)
- ¼ medium onion (peeled: 1 ounce)
- 8 sprigs parsley (including stems: ½ ounce)
- 1 fresh jalapeño pepper (seeded: ¼ ounce or to taste)
- 1 small garlic clove (peeled)
- 1 medium tomato (6 ounces)

Juice in the order of the listed ingredients.

Makes about 1 cup

V-4

- 3 to 4 clumps spinach (trimmed: 4 ounces)
- ¼ medium red pepper (stem, pith, and seeds removed: 4 ounces)
- 1 small tomato (4 ounces)
- 1 large carrot (top trimmed: 6 ounces)

Juice in the order of the listed ingredients.

Makes about 1 cup

Gazpacho

- 1½-inch green pepper wedge (1 ounce)
- 1¼-inch onion wedge (½ ounce)
- 1 small tomato (4 ounces)
- ½ medium cucumber (peeled if waxed: 3½ ounces)

Juice in the order of the listed ingredients.

Makes about 1 cup

128

V-6

- 1 small tomato (4 ounces)
- 1 large outer celery rib (trimmed: 3 ounces)
- ½ medium cucumber (peeled if waxed: 3½ ounces)
- 1 small carrot (top trimmed: 2 ounces)
- 1 small beet (trimmed: 2 ounces)
- 4 sprigs parsley (stems included: ¼ ounce)
- Celery salt to taste (optional)

Juice in the order of the listed ingredients. Stir in celery salt, if using.

Makes about ¾ cup

Fruit and Vegetable Combinations

Day Breaker

- 1 large carrot (trimmed: 6 ounces)
- 1 medium juice orange (peeled and seeded: 5 ounces)

Juice in the order of the listed ingredients.

Makes about ⅔ cup

Apple-Beet Energizer

- 1 large McIntosh apple (cored: 8 ounces)
- 1 medium beet (trimmed: 4 ounces)

Juice in the order of the listed ingredients.

Makes about ¾ cup

Cool as a Strawberry

- 6 large strawberries (hulled: 6 ounces)
- ½ medium cucumber (peeled if waxed: 3½ ounces)

Juice in the order of the listed ingredients.

Makes about ¾ cup

Spinach-Apple Squash

- 2 to 3 medium clumps spinach (bottoms trimmed: 3 ounces)
- 1 medium Golden Delicious apple (cored: 6 ounces)

Juice in the order of the listed ingredients.

Makes about ¾ cup

Tomato Surprise

- 1 small tomato (4 ounces)
- ¼ small cantaloupe (seeds and rind removed: 4 ounces)

Juice in the order of the listed ingredients.

Makes about ½ cup

Carrot Patch

131

- 6 large strawberries (hulled: 6 ounces)
- 1 large carrot (top trimmed: 6 ounces)

Juice in the order of the listed ingredients.

Makes about ¾ cup

Golden Fennel

- 1 small fennel bulb (leaves and stalks discarded: 4 ounces)
- 1 large Golden Delicious apple (cored: 8 ounces)

Juice in the order of the listed ingredients.

Makes about ¾ cup

132 ### Hawaiian Carrot Juice

- ¼ pineapple (rind removed: 7 ounces)
- 1 medium carrot (top trimmed: 4 ounces)

Juice in the order of the listed ingredients.

Makes about ⅔ cup

Spinach Sunshine

- 2 to 3 large clumps spinach (bottoms trimmed: 3 ounces)
- 2 medium juice oranges (peeled and seeded: 5 ounces each)

Juice in the order of the listed ingredients.

Makes about ¾ cup

Pineapple-Celery Refresher

133

- ¼ pineapple (rind removed: 7 ounces)
- 2 large outer celery ribs (tops and bottoms trimmed: 6 ounces)

Juice in the order of the listed ingredients.

Makes about ¾ cup

Throat-Tingling Hot Apple Juice

- 3 medium red radishes (leaves and root removed: 2 ounces)
- 1 medium Golden Delicious apple (cored: 6 ounces)

Juice in the order of the listed ingredients.

Makes about ⅔ cup

Mango Tango

- ½ mango (peeled and pitted: 3 ounces)
- 2 medium apricots (pitted: 1½ ounces each)
- 1 large carrot (top trimmed: 6 ounces)

Juice in the order of the listed ingredients.

Makes about ⅔ cup

Heavenly Cherry-Beet and Orange Juice

- 10 medium cherries (stemmed and pitted: 2 ounces)
- 1 medium beet (trimmed: 4 ounces)
- 1 medium juice orange (peeled and seeded: 5 ounces)

Juice in the order of the listed ingredients.

Makes about ¾ cup

Blackberry-Celery Quencher

- ⅓ cup blackberries (2 ounces)
- ½ medium apple (cored: 3 ounces)
- 2 medium celery ribs (trimmed: 4 ounces)

Juice in the order of the listed ingredients.

Makes about ⅔ cup

Carrot-Kohlrabi-Can't Elope

- ¼ small cantaloupe (seeds and rind removed: 3 ounces)
- 1 large carrot (top trimmed: 6 ounces)
- 1 medium kohlrabi (trimmed: 4 ounces)

Juice in the order of the listed ingredients.

Makes about ¾ cup

Super "A" Delight

136

- 1 mango (peeled and seeded: 6 ounces)
- 1 medium peach (seeded: 6 ounces)
- 1 large carrot (top trimmed: 6 ounces)

Juice in the order of the listed ingredients.

Makes about 1 cup

Asparagus-Cucumber Cooler

- 4 medium asparagus (bottoms trimmed: 2 ounces)
- ½ medium cucumber (peeled if waxed: 3½ ounces)
- ¼ large apple (seeded: 2 ounces)

Juice in the order of the listed ingredients.

Makes about ¾ cup

Fruity Tonic

- ¼ pineapple (rind removed: 7 ounces)
- ¼ large Golden Delicious apple (cored: 2 ounces)
- 2 large outer celery ribs (trimmed: 6 ounces)

Juice in the order of the listed ingredients.

Makes about 1 cup

Magenta Madness

- 25 small seedless green grapes (stems removed: 3 ounces)
- 6 large strawberries (hulled: 6 ounces)
- 1 medium beet (top and bottom trimmed: 4 ounces)

Juice in the order of the listed ingredients.

Makes about ⅔ cup

Celery Soother

- 1 medium ripe pear (stemmed and cored: 6 ounces)
- 10 large seedless green grapes (stems removed: 2 ounces)
- 2 large outer celery ribs (trimmed: 6 ounces)

Juice in the order of the listed ingredients.

Makes about 1 cup

Carrot Caper

- 7 medium strawberries (hulled: 4 ounces)
- 1 medium carrot (top trimmed: 4 ounces)
- 1 thin pineapple wedge (rind removed: 2 ounces)

Juice in the order of the listed ingredients.

Makes about ¾ cup

Honeydew Refresher

139

- 10 large seedless green grapes (stems removed: 2 ounces)
- ⅙ honeydew (seeds and rind removed: 8 ounces)
- ½ small cucumber (peeled if waxed: 3½ ounces)

Juice in the order of the listed ingredients.

Makes about 1 cup

Cabbage Patch

- 1 small wedge cabbage (3 ounces)
- 1 large outer celery rib (trimmed: 3 ounces)
- ¼ large Golden Delicious apple (cored: 2 ounces)

Juice in the order of the listed ingredients.

Makes about ½ cup

140

Purple Punch

- ¾ cup blackberries (4 ounces)
- 1 medium juice orange (peeled and seeded: 5 ounces)
- 1 medium beet (trimmed: 4 ounces)

Juice in the order of the listed ingredients.

Makes about ⅔ cup

Green Fiend

- 2 to 3 clumps spinach (bottoms trimmed: 3 ounces)
- ⅛ pineapple (rind removed: 3½ ounces)
- ½ medium Golden Delicious apple (cored: 3 ounces)
- ½ medium cucumber (peeled if waxed: 3½ ounces)

Juice in the order of the listed ingredients.

Makes about 1 cup

Fruity Beet Cocktail

- ¼ medium banana (peeled: 1½ ounces)
- 2 small apricots (pitted: 2 ounces)
- 1 small plum (pitted: 2 ounces)
- 10 large green grapes (stems removed: 2 ounces)
- 1 medium beet (trimmed: 4 ounces)

Juice in the order of the listed ingredients.

Makes about ¾ cup

Minty Refresher

- 1 large kiwi (peeled: 3 ounces)
- 4 sprigs fresh mint
- ½ medium grapefruit (peeled and seeded: 3½ ounces)
- 2 large celery ribs (trimmed: 6 ounces)

Juice in the order of the listed ingredients.

Makes about 1 cup

Vege-Fruit Cocktail

- 1 to 2 large clumps spinach (bottoms trimmed: 2 ounces)
- 3 large strawberries (hulled: 3 ounces)
- ½ large Golden Delicious apple (cored: 4 ounces)
- ½ medium cucumber (peeled if waxed: 3½ ounces)

Juice in the order of the listed ingredients.

Makes about ¾ cup

Rooty-Fruity

- 1 medium nectarine (pitted: 4 ounces)
- 4 large strawberries (hulled: 4 ounces)
- 1 medium carrot (top trimmed: 4 ounces)
- 1 small beet (trimmed: 2 ounces)

Juice in the order of the listed ingredients.

Makes about 1 cup

143

Fennel-Vege-Pear Combo

- 1 small fennel bulb (leaves and stalks discarded: 4 ounces)
- ½ large ripe pear (stemmed and seeded: 3 ounces)
- 3 to 4 clumps spinach (trimmed: 4 ounces)
- 1 medium celery rib (trimmed: 2 ounces)

Juice in the order of the listed ingredients.

Makes about ¾ cup

Blender Drinks

Drinks prepared in the blender have the advantage of including all the fruit's nutrients and fiber. Dairy and soybean products, which provide high protein contents, can also be incorporated.

When juice is called for in the blender recipes, you can use prepared or fresh juices.

The blender can purée only soft fruits with soft skins; if you want to use peaches or nectarines, they must be ripe to blend. Bananas and ripe strawberries are ideal blender ingredients. You will get a smoother drink if you purée the fruits before you add any liquid.

Nectarine-Orange Smoothie

- 1 large ripe nectarine, cut into chunks (pitted: 5½ ounces)
- ½ cup orange juice

With the blender running, put the nectarine chunks through the hole in the lid. Process until the nectarine is puréed. Add the orange juice and process until combined.

Makes about 1 cup

Strawberry-Pineapple Smoothie

- 4 large strawberries (hulled: 4 ounces)
- ⅛ pineapple (rind and core removed and cut into chunks: 3½ ounces)
- Sweetener to taste (optional)

With the blender running, put the strawberries through the hole in the lid. Blend until the strawberries are puréed. Add the pineapple chunks through the hole while the blender is running. When mixture is smooth, add optional sweetener.

Makes about ¾ cup

Apple-Honeydew Smash

- 1½-inch wedge honeydew melon (rind removed and cut into chunks: 4 ounces)
- ⅓ cup apple juice

Place the honeydew in a blender. Cover and blend until puréed. Add the apple juice. Cover and process until smooth.

Makes about ¾ cup

147

Strawberry-Orange Pick-Me-Up

- 4 large strawberries (hulled: 4 ounces)
- ½ cup orange juice

With the blender running, put the strawberries through the hole in the lid. Process until the strawberries are puréed. Add the orange juice and blend until combined.

Makes about 1 cup

Mango Lassi (Indian Yogurt Drink)*

- ½ ripe mango (peeled, pitted, and cut into chunks: 4 ounces)
- ⅓ cup unflavored yogurt

Place the mango and yogurt in a blender. Cover and blend until smooth.

Makes about ¾ cup

* You can use a variety of fruits for this tangy drink; nectarine, peach, cantaloupe, or strawberry are all good.

Strawberry Milk Shake

- 4 large strawberries (hulled: 4 ounces)
- ½ cup milk (dairy or soy)
- Sweetener to taste (optional)

With the blender running, put the strawberries through the hole in the lid. Blend until the strawberries are puréed. Add the milk and sweetener; blend until smooth.

Makes about 1 cup

Blueberry Flip

- ½ cup fresh blueberries (3 ounces)*
- ½ cup milk (dairy or soy)
- 2 to 3 ice cubes
- Sweetener to taste (optional)

Place the blueberries and milk in a blender. Cover and process until smooth. Add ice cubes and sweetener, if using, and process until smooth.

Makes about 1 cup

149

* You can use frozen blueberries and eliminate the ice cubes.

Frozen Banana Shake

- 5 one-inch chunks frozen banana (peeled: 4 ounces)
- ½ cup milk (dairy or soy)
- Sweetener to taste (optional)

Place the banana, milk, and sweetener in a blender. Cover and blend until smooth.

Makes about 1 cup

These two blender drinks were developed at La Costa Spa in California:

Cran-Raspberry Juice

- 9 ounces cranberry juice
- ¼ cup fresh raspberries (1½ ounces)

Place juice and raspberries in a blender. Cover and process until smooth.

Serves 2 to 3

Tropical Blend Juice

- 6 ounces pineapple juice
- ¼ papaya (peeled and seeded: 2½ ounces)
- ¼ banana (peeled: 1 ounce)
- 2 tablespoons water

Place all ingredients in a blender. Cover and process until smooth.

Serves 2 to 3

The following drinks are from the Doral Saturnia International Spa Resort in Florida:

Pineapple Mint Slush

- ½ cup fresh pineapple chunks
- ¼ cucumber (peeled and seeded: 2½ ounces)
- 1 tablespoon fresh lime juice
- 2 to 3 mint leaves
- 1 cup ice cubes

Place the pineapple, cucumber, lime juice, and mint in a blender. Cover and blend 5 seconds. Add ice, cover, and blend until smooth.

Serves 1 to 2

Orange Papaya Slush

- ½ ripe papaya (peeled and seeded: 8 ounces)
- 1 cup fresh orange juice
- 1 cup ice cubes

Place all ingredients in a blender. Cover and blend until smooth.

Serves 3

The Spa at Palm-Aire developed this drink:

Banana Shake

- ½ very ripe banana (peeled: 2 ounces)
- ½ cup skim milk
- 1½ teaspoons nonfat dry milk
- 1 to 2 ice cubes

Place all ingredients in a blender. Cover and blend until smooth.

Serves 1 to 2

Waste Not, Want Not

Everyone who owns a juice extractor wonders what to do with the pulp. It seems too good to throw away or add to the compost heap. The recipes that follow were developed to use all that nutritious pulp.

Accumulate pulp from one, two, or three days' worth of juicing and save it in the refrigerator or freezer, taking care to keep the fruit and vegetable pulp separate. Defrost frozen pulp before using it.

Frozen Fruit Pops or Cubes

This works best with pulp from soft fruits or a combination of soft and hard fruits. For best results, plain apple and/or orange pulp should be blended with softer fruits such as mangoes, peaches, pears, or berries.

If you don't have ice pop sticks, you can make just cubes, which you can use as a snack or for Fruity Gelatin, Fruity Iced Tea, or Fruity Shakes.

• Fruit pulp
• Sugar or sweetener to taste, if desired

154

Stir the fruit pulp and sugar together.

If you have made a large batch of juice, and have ice pop forms and sticks, just spoon in the fruit pulp and freeze as you would any ice pop.

If you have just a little pulp, spoon it into an ice cube tray. For ice pops when the cube is partially frozen, stand a wooden stick in the center. Let freeze completely. If making fruit cubes without the sticks, you may need to pry them out of the ice cube tray with the tip of a sharp knife.

Fruity Gelatin

In addition to giving a fresh fruit flavor to the packaged mixes, Frozen Fruit Cubes add great fiber to a dessert that is usually devoid of any nutritional value. They also help the gelatin set sooner by cooling the mixture.

Be sure the Frozen Fruit Cubes have no pineapple or kiwi in them because those fruits contain enzymes that prevent the gelatin from setting.

- 1 package fruit-flavored gelatin (regular or low-calorie)
- 2 cups boiling water
- 2 or more Frozen Fruit Cubes (opposite page)

155

Add the gelatin to the boiling water, stirring until the gelatin dissolves. Add fruit cubes and stir until they dissolve. When the gelatin is half set, stir it so the pulp is evenly dispersed and doesn't just sit on the bottom. Let set completely.

Serves 4

Fruit Juice Gelatin

You can use any bottled or fresh juice except fresh pineapple or kiwi juice or pulp because these fruits contain enzymes that prevent the gelatin from setting. You can also use vegetable juice and pulp to make this into an aspic.

- 1 package unflavored gelatin
- ½ cup water
- 3 Frozen Fruit Cubes (page 154)
- 1¼ cups fruit juice

156

In a medium saucepan, stir the gelatin into the water and let stand 5 minutes, until the gelatin is softened. Cook, stirring, over medium heat until the mixture is hot and small bubbles form around the edge of the liquid. Remove from heat and stir in the Frozen Fruit Cubes. When they dissolve, stir in the juice. Pour into dessert cups or a 3-cup mold and chill.

Serves 4

Microwave variation: Stir the gelatin into water in a 2-cup glass measuring cup. Let stand until gelatin is softened. Microwave on high (100%) power 1 minute. Stir in the Frozen Fruit Cubes and the juice. Pour into dessert cups or mold. Let chill.

Fruity Iced Tea

By the end of the summer I've usually had so much iced tea I'm tired of the flavor. By adding Frozen Fruit Cubes to my iced tea I'm no longer bored.

- 6 to 8 ounces cold tea
- Sweetener to taste
- 4 ice cubes
- 1 Frozen Fruit Cube (page 154)

Pour the cold tea into a large glass. Sweeten to taste and add the ice and Frozen Fruit Cube.

Serves 1

157

Fruity Shake

You can use whole or skim milk or fruit juice. I use an old-fashioned ice cube tray that makes fairly large cubes, so I use only two in this shake.

- ½ cup milk or juice
- 2 to 3 Frozen Fruit Cubes (page 154)

Place all ingredients in a blender. Cover and blend until thick and smooth.

Serves 1

Beet, Carrot, and Orange Bread

This delicious quick bread is best if left overnight to mellow before serving. It's great spread with jam and it also freezes well (slice first). You can use just beet or carrot pulp, if you prefer.

- 1¾ cups all-purpose flour
- ¾ cup whole wheat flour
- 1 teaspoon baking powder
- 1 teaspoon baking soda
- ½ teaspoon salt
- ¾ cup vegetable oil
- ½ cup orange juice
- 4 egg whites
- 1½ cups sugar
- ½ cup carrot pulp
- ½ cup beet pulp
- 1 tablespoon grated orange peel
- 2 teaspoons vanilla extract

Preheat the oven to 350° F. Heavily grease and flour a 9 x 5 x 3-inch loaf pan; set aside.

In a large bowl, or on a piece of wax paper, whisk together the two types of flour, baking powder, baking soda, and salt; set aside.

In a large bowl, beat together the oil, orange juice, and egg whites until combined. Add the sugar, carrot and beet pulps, orange peel, and vanilla extract. Beat until combined.

Add the flour mixture and beat until just combined. Spoon into prepared loaf pan and bake 1 hour 10 minutes, or until a wooden pick inserted into the center of the loaf comes out clean. Let cool in pan 15 minutes before turning onto rack to cool completely. Wrap in aluminum foil and let stand overnight.

Serves 10 to 12

Hi-Fi Carrot Cake

- 1 cup all-purpose flour
- ½ cup oat bran
- 2 teaspoons ground cinnamon
- 1½ teaspoons baking powder
- 1 teaspoon baking soda
- ½ teaspoon salt
- ½ cup sugar
- ½ cup firmly packed light or dark brown sugar
- ½ cup vegetable oil
- 3 egg whites
- 1 teaspoon vanilla extract
- 1 can (8½ ounces) crushed pineapple, with juice
- 1 cup lightly packed carrot pulp

160

Preheat the oven to 350° F. Heavily grease and flour a 9 x 5 x 3-inch loaf pan; set aside.

In a large bowl, or on a piece of wax paper, whisk together the flour, oat bran, cinnamon, baking powder, baking soda, and salt.

In a large bowl, using an electric mixer, beat together both sugars, oil, egg whites, and vanilla until combined. Stir in the pineapple with the juice and carrot pulp.

Add the flour mixture to the carrot mixture and stir until combined. Spoon into prepared loaf pan.

Bake 55 minutes, or until a wooden pick inserted in the center comes out clean. Turn onto a wire rack to cool completely.

Serves 12

Carrot Pulp Muffins

- 1 cup all-purpose flour
- ½ cup whole wheat flour
- 2 teaspoons baking powder
- 1 teaspoon baking soda
- ½ teaspoon salt
- ¼ teaspoon grated nutmeg
- ¼ cup shortening
- 3 tablespoons light or dark brown sugar
- 1 egg
- 1 cup buttermilk
- ¾ cup carrot pulp
- 3 tablespoons honey

161

Preheat the oven to 400° F. Grease 12 (2½-inch) muffin cups.

In a large bowl, or on a piece of wax paper, whisk together both flours, baking powder, baking soda, salt, and nutmeg; set aside.

In a large bowl, cream the shortening with the sugar. Beat in the egg, then the buttermilk, carrot pulp, and honey. Add the dry ingredients, stirring just until combined, but still lumpy.

Spoon into the prepared muffin cups (they will be quite full). Bake 20 minutes, or until a wooden pick inserted in the center comes out clean.

Makes 12 muffins

Vegetable Broth

One problem for vegetarian cooks is that there are not any good ready-made substitutes for chicken broth. If you want to have good vegetarian broth, you have to make it from scratch and that can be expensive and time consuming. My solution is to make broth from leftover pulp. It's easy and costs virtually nothing, since you would probably have thrown the pulp away. The broth can be refrigerated for 4 or 5 days or frozen for several months.

- 6 cups water
- 3 cups vegetable pulp
- ½ onion
- 1 garlic clove, left whole
- Parsley, celery leaves, or dill
- Salt to taste

Place the water, pulp, onion, garlic, and parsley in a 3-quart saucepan. Bring to a boil over high heat. Reduce heat and simmer 45 minutes, uncovered.

Place a fine mesh strainer over a large bowl. Pour 1 cup of the broth-pulp mixture into the strainer. Using the back of a glass, press the liquid out of the pulp. Discard the pulp and repeat with another cup of the broth-pulp mixture until all the broth has been drained into the bowl and the pulp discarded. Add salt to taste.

Makes about 3 cups

Cream of (Almost) Anything Soup

This is not really quite suited for *any*thing, because it won't work with fruit or very stringy pulp. But if you have pulp from broccoli, cauliflower, spinach, or other flavorful vegetables, try them here. This is also an ideal use for vegetable broth.

- 2 tablespoons butter or margarine
- 1 tablespoon minced shallots
- 2 tablespoons flour
- 3 cups vegetable or chicken broth
- 1 cup vegetable pulp
- ¾ cup cream or milk

In a 3-quart saucepan, heat the butter over medium-high heat. Stir in the shallots and cook until slightly transparent. Stir in the flour until absorbed. Using a wire whisk, stir in the broth until smooth. Add the pulp and cook, stirring, until mixture comes to a boil. Remove from heat and stir in the cream.

163

Serves 4 to 6

BIBLIOGRAPHY

Bricklin, Mark. *Rodale's Encyclopedia of Natural Home Remedies.* Emmaus, Pa.: Rodale Press, 1982.

Calbom, Cherie, and Maureen Keane. *Juicing for Life—A Guide to the Health Benefits of Fresh Fruit and Vegetable Juicing.* Garden City Park, N.Y.: Avery Publishing Group Inc., 1992.

Hillman, Howard. *The Cook's Book.* New York: Avon, 1981.

Kordich, Jay. *The Juiceman's Power of Juicing.* New York: William Morrow and Company Inc., 1992.

National Research Council. *Recommended Dietary Allowances.* 10th ed. Washington, D.C.: National Academy Press, 1989.

Townsend, Doris McFerran. *The Cook's Companion.* New York: Crown Publishers, Inc. 1978.

Walker, N. W. *Fresh Vegetable and Fruit Juices—What's Missing in Your Body?* Prescott, Ariz.: Norwalk Press, 1978.

Whitney, Eleanor Noss, Eva May Nunnelley Hamilton, and Sharon Rady Rolfes. *Understanding Nutrition.* 5th ed. St. Paul, Minn.: West Publishing Company, 1990.

Wilen, Joan, and Lydia Wilen. *More Chicken Soup and Other Folk Remedies.* New York: Fawcett Columbine, 1986.

Lee, William H. *The Book of Raw Fruit and Vegetable Juices and Drinks.* New Canaan, Conn.: Keats Publishing, Inc., 1982.

INDEX